"The mysteries of God cannot always be explained except in paradoxes. Tom Taylor's new book, *Paradoxy: Coming to Grips with the Contradictions of Jesus*, is a book with a WOW message for every Christian and for those who have never understood the apparent contradictions of Jesus. Tom Taylor's insights in *Paradoxy* clearly reveal how Jesus's upside-down view of life can turn us right side up . . . read it!"

Robert H. Schuller, founder, Crystal Cathedral Ministries

"The tension of paradox is something few of us choose to engage. Tom Taylor brilliantly leads the reader through compelling story to the power of Jesus and his paradoxes that both promise and deliver on peace. Few things are needed more today than such a reminder."

Nancy Murphy, associate professor, Mars Hill Graduate School; executive director, Northwest Family Life

"Tom Taylor retrieves the message of Jesus with wit and wisdom."

Allen Verhey, professor of Christian ethics, Duke Divinity School

"In an era of so many Christian books to choose from, it becomes difficult to know which books are really going to be helpful and which are not. This book is one of those books you really must choose because it is not only helpful but life changing. Once you begin to see, as the author so clearly explains, that life is full of paradox—and that Jesus knew this and taught this—you will never again be tempted to make life clean and simple. Tom's writing style reminds me of the writings of Donald Miller and Anne Lamott—fresh and honest and funny and not afraid to be human, while at the same time committed to his Christian convictions. This book is not afraid to tackle life's most difficult questions—*Why am I here? How do I find fulfillment?*—and it does so with grace and insight. This may well be the best book you read this year. I know it is the best book I have *ever* read on the difficult teachings of Jesus."

James Bryan Smith, author, *Embracing the Love of God*; coauthor with Richard J. Foster, *Devotional Classics*

a seeming contradiction

PARADOXY

Coming to Grips with the
Contradictions of Jesus

oxymoron
a pointedly foolish contradiction   benevolent dictator

TOM TAYLOR

BakerBooks
Grand Rapids, Michigan

Published by Baker Books
a division of Baker Publishing Group
P.O. Box 6287, Grand Rapids, MI 49516-6287
www.bakerbooks.com

Printed in the United States of America

Library of Congress Cataloging-in-Publication Data
Taylor, Thomas F., 1959–
        Paradoxy : coming to grips with the contradictions of Jesus / Tom Taylor.
            p.   cm.
        Includes bibliographical references.
        ISBN 10: 0-8010-6539-9 (pbk.)
        ISBN 978-0-8010-6539-2 (pbk.)
        1. Jesus Christ—Teachings. 2. Christian life—Biblical teaching. I. Title.
        BS2415.T39 2006
        232.9′54—dc22   2006001713

For my brother, Tim—
whose honesty about a faith that he does not confess
has compelled me to clarify one that I cannot deny.

Contents

Prologue

If you had hung around Jesus for three years, as his closest disciples did, what would you have come away with? Certainly you would have come to know the upside-down way that Jesus saw the world. Jesus taught that we experience God in counterintuitive ways.

This book is about learning to see life through Jesus' eyes. It is not a book mainly of ethics and morals. It is about taking on a new worldview. In his intentionally overturned vision, Jesus offered something that we all desperately long for—inward peace.

1: Peace for Restless Souls

The great paradox of the 21st century is that, in this age of powerful technology, the biggest problems we face internationally are problems of the human soul.

Ralph Peters

It is the paradox of life that the way to miss pleasure is to seek it first.

Hugo Black

Restlessness is an ache of our age. But our deep, unmet desire for personal peace is nothing new. The ancient Greek philosophers were restless to understand how the world works and why we exist. On the other side of the world, Buddha taught that life is suffering precisely because humans are not at peace; we lack peace, Buddha said, because we engage in undisciplined worldly passions and attachments. Today, gurus and hucksters fill our airwaves hawking CDs, seminars, and autographed pictures of Jesus, claiming that they will bring immediate personal peace in five easy steps and three easy payments. For those who know the pain and struggle of an authentic search for peace, such claims are painful even to hear.

If most of us were honest, we'd have to admit that it's our heart's deep desire to have personal peace, even in the midst of life's unrest. Life is full of things that tempt us toward or create trouble. We get divorced when we always thought, *Not my marriage.* Our children commit crimes, our taxes get audited, our workplaces implode, our investments deplete, our girlfriends or boyfriends break our hearts, our nations wage wars, our lives turn messy. We experience incredible strife that leads to discouragement and anxiety. And where is God in all of this?

I am the son of a pastor, raised among conservative Christian evangelicals in the American Midwest. Although I practiced as an attorney for two large law firms, much of my adult career has been as a Christian minister. Yet in all these years of interaction with Christianity, one particular Christian ideal has seemed troublingly elusive—so-called personal peace.

Jesus of Nazareth promised his followers profound personal peace: "Peace I leave with you," he said; "my peace I give you. I do not give to you as the world gives. Do not let your hearts be troubled and do not be afraid" (John 14:27). Biblical authors who followed Jesus found the peace that he promised. St. Paul—often referred to as the second founder of Christianity—explained to a group of early Christians in a city called Philippi, "Whatever you have learned or received or heard from me, or seen in me—put it into practice. And the God of peace will be with you" (Phil. 4:9). Paul's journey of peace with God became so real that he boldly commanded others to find it by following his own example; they too could experience the same peace.

PARADOXY

Regrettably, I don't know many Christians who have found this peace of God. I know many dozens of Christians for whom I have great love and respect, who have demonstrated compassion for others, deep humility, and sage-like wisdom. But even among the most admirable and Christlike individuals I have met, few seem to live with that deep, personal peace that the Bible speaks so much of—the peace that would seem to be a natural result of a "personal relationship with God." Fewer still say to others with Paul's boldness, "You can find God's peace just as I have." Those who do say such things more often seem to be full of self-grandeur, not divine peace.

I have found another frustrating contradiction in the Christian world. Jesus described the peace of God as different from anything the world has to offer. St. Paul similarly said, "The peace of God . . . transcends all understanding" (Phil. 4:7). Yet many Christians appear to recommend—as I think the secular world does—a formulaic version of peace, based on acquiring the right knowledge. If we just get the right answers to questions such as, "Does God exist?" or "Is the Christian God the one true God?" or "Why does an all-powerful, all-loving God allow suffering?" then we can find peace. These are important questions, but would having the answers really bring peace when the questions arise from the pain of our own bewildering circumstances? Sound theology and accurate thought processes are helpful. But does God's peace come by knowing the right answers? I don't think so. We can have all the right information and the best understanding of Christian doctrine and still experience great pain, loneliness, and inner unrest. Even Scripture makes it clear that God's true peace is beyond the grip of human comprehension.

Someone said, "If at first you don't succeed, skydiving is definitely not for you." Success does not always come by trying harder. Believers and seekers alike often miss the secret of Jesus' teachings about God's peace. We think in terms of fixing things, getting it right, following the right steps in the right order. But Jesus taught that when our pictures don't look straight, God is often inviting us to enjoy them in their crookedness. Instead of begging God to change our circumstances, we should roll up our sleeves and dive into them just as they are, because we are right where God wants us to be. It is on crooked paths, in unwanted circumstances, that we find God's plans for us—and some of the greatest things that life has to offer.

Finding Peace Where You Least Expect It

St. Paul's personal conversion radically altered his life. In his younger years, he was a systematic serial killer of Christians. By the end of his life, he had transformed the Mediterranean world for the cause of Jesus Christ.

What caused such a profound change? Was it having the right knowledge—the right answers? Was it some theological genius or special spiritual information? Hardly. In fact, despite his profound spiritual knowledge, Paul freely admitted, "Now we see but a poor reflection as in a mirror. . . . Now I know in part" (1 Cor. 13:12). Paul's peace came not by knowing all the answers but while he lived without them.

We tend to misunderstand Jesus' teachings about the qualities of personal peace, such as rest, gratification, freedom, and the like, in part because much of it was *paradox*—a truth that appears to contradict itself. We want things spelled out nice and clear, unmistakably. We have trouble with paradox because it makes a claim that appears to be the opposite of what we think is true.

PARADOXY

"The only constant is change."

"Standing is more tiring than walking."

"Youth is wasted on the young."

In their irony, paradoxes display the inherent tensions of everyday life. They reveal how we are often torn in our decisions or actions. Some mistakenly characterize paradoxes as mere contradictions. Others dismiss them as anomalies we can't explain. But neither of these accurately captures their essence. Paradoxes are potent statements about realities, not because they are mysterious or clever, but because they are true.

Upon receiving the Broadcaster of the Year Award, *Nightline* news anchor Ted Koppel said, "Consider this paradox: Almost everything that is publicly said these days is recorded. Almost nothing of what is said is worth remembering."[1] A paradox is a truth that bites its own tail.

If nothing else, the paradoxes of Jesus clearly reveal that he understood and empathized with our emotional, physical, and spiritual struggles. Jesus knows that we frequently drive ourselves to depression in our pursuit of perpetual happiness. We are often cruelest and most indifferent toward those we love most. We crave fame until we attain it, and then we flee into solitude. We neurotically worry and insure against catastrophes to calm ourselves against accidents that rarely occur. We climb the pole of power only to find it is greasiest at the top. We continually plan days, months, and years ahead, only to find at the end of life that we were chasing the end of the rainbow. The real magic we sought was there all along, in those everyday relationships and ordinary events that we took for granted.

A Train to Yonkers

Growing up in a Christian minister's home was in some ways a paradox for me. In our church, I enjoyed all the glory and suffered all the misery of being the center of attention. Church people can be ruthless. I suspect that their critical scrutiny is one reason so many pastors' kids go through a faith crisis by the time they reach early adulthood.

I experienced that kind of faith crisis in my early twenties. I was living in a state of personal unrest. My inner turmoil involved not only serious doubts about my faith but also questions like which career path to choose, why my relationships with women never worked out, and how far I should step over moral boundaries. I had not only lost a sense of God, I had lost a sense of my self. I had lost my moorings.

My faith crisis and general unrest were serious enough that I thought I should treat them with a master's degree from Yale Divinity School. My studies were of little help. The insights and care of several friends and mentors helped some. But throughout those years, my only real source of healing and growth came from God.

During one particular period in my graduate studies, my doubts about God reached an extreme. I had a laundry list: I doubted God's love. I doubted God's power. At times I even doubted God's existence. The problem was not that I didn't have enough intellectual information about God. In fact, I think I had heard too much that had long since become hollow. The answers to my many questions were not *my* answers. I did not own them in my heart; they did not lead me to sense God or his presence in the ways that I so deeply wanted and needed. Not surprisingly, personal peace eluded me.

PARADOXY

On a cold November day during that time, I was returning to Yale's divinity school in New Haven, Connecticut, after visiting my brother in New York City. I got on the train and lumbered to my seat. I gazed out the window as we left behind the jostling crowds on the platform and the loud, high-pitched screech and hiss of trains pulling in and out of the station. I felt so lonely. I wanted life to have some meaning beyond my small pursuits and the mundane world around me. But I was in a state of grave doubt that such meaning really existed, or if it did, that a person could know it.

As our train picked up speed and the rhythm of the tracks beneath us began to lull me into some relaxation, I noticed a young Asian man in his early twenties sitting across from me. He had that deliberately unkempt look of a student, but instead of the overly confident or indifferent expression of so many graduate students, he was crying. As our ride progressed, I realized he wasn't just crying. He was sobbing almost uncontrollably.

I was moved to talk to him. I went over to him and sat next to him, asking if I could help. He didn't speak English. I used fragments of the few languages I knew to try to communicate, but was only able to learn a few things. He was from China—Beijing. He was so deeply upset because a loved one had died. Just when I thought his situation was as bad as it could get, I looked down at his ticket and noticed he was on the wrong train. His ticket was to Yonkers, but he had left Grand Central in another direction: on the New Haven line, not the Hudson.

Using little more than hand and head gestures and intonation, I was able to convey to him that he was on the wrong train. I told this to one of the train car conductors who expressed all the compassion of an exhausted bureaucrat. Without taking his eyes off the tickets he was punching, he shouted crabbily above the train noise, "He'll have to get off at the next stop and get on the right train."

Brilliant! I thought. *What a compassionate guy.* I motioned for my new friend to sit tight until the next stop, where I would try to help him.

I went back and slumped into my seat. Seeing this young guy's predicament somehow magnified my jaded and frustrated feelings about God. I'll never forget my prayer. Though I believed in God's existence, at that moment I certainly doubted God's goodness. I prayed, "God, why do you let people go through this kind of stuff? Why don't you cut this guy some slack?!"

We were some ways out of Grand Central, and the first stop was Greenwich, Connecticut, an Eastern township not known for its folksy compassion. I didn't expect much help from its residents. I had only minutes while the doors were open to convey to my grieving, bewildered, non-English-speaking friend that he needed to get off the train, go underneath the tracks and up onto the opposing platform, explain to a conductor that he had to take the train back to Grand Central, and then catch the right train to Yonkers.

Our train stopped. I motioned for the guy to get up and come with me. I took him by the arm to the door, which opened with a thud. *This is hopeless*, I thought. Just then, I saw a pleasant albeit rather stiff-looking woman standing there on the platform just a few feet outside the door.

I said, "Ma'am, I have a situation here. Could you help us?"

Cautiously, she said, "Maybe, what is it?" I gently nudged my friend out of the car toward her and explained the situation as quickly and completely as I could. As I talked, she appeared more and more puzzled. I had a sinking feeling as her puzzlement

PARADOXY

turned to downright perplexity. Time was running out before the doors would close.

"Ma'am, is there a problem?" I asked impatiently. "Are you getting this?"

She said, "Well, this is just so odd. I mean, this poor guy is so far from home and doesn't speak any English—only Chinese. And I am about to meet my old college roommate right here on this platform whom I haven't seen for twenty years, and she is from China." Just then, a smiling Asian woman came up and hugged the woman, then looked immediately at my sad friend with great compassion and began to speak to him in Cantonese. He began to sob with what was obviously great relief, and she put her arm around him. The first woman looked at me, beaming with a smile that I couldn't return. Stunned, I stepped back onto the train. The doors closed in my face, and the three drifted past my windows like a movie that I was watching from a distance. I never saw them again.

I returned to my seat. What had just happened? *How* had that happened? Suddenly, I recalled that I had asked God to cut this sojourner some slack. I instantly began to sense God's presence and a personal peace in a powerful and very real way. I had asked with such contempt and bitterness for God's help, but somehow I knew that God had intervened with grace and generosity. My skeptical side desperately wanted to enter the fray. But could I say with any sense of personal integrity, "Gee, what a coincidence"? The words of a friend of mine from years earlier came to mind. "When God enters your time and space," he said, "there is always room for the possibility that it is something other than God. But then, there will always be the possibility that it *is* God."

It was like so many of the paradoxes I had come across in Jesus' teachings. In the tension of my doubt and sadness, I experienced at that moment a profound sense of personal peace. In the jostling confusion of a public train, I presumed that God looked on from far away with indifference. But to the contrary, I saw God's kindness. And I knew that day, in that quiet miracle, God was there with us.

The Paradoxes of Jesus

The book of Luke records that one dusty Middle Eastern day Jesus was traveling from the north of Palestine south toward Jerusalem, making his way through each village as he went. In one town some aristocratic religious leaders approached him and asked when the kingdom of God would come. Jesus answered their question: "The kingdom of God is not coming with things that can be observed" (17:20 NRSV). Then, rather strangely, he directed his answer not to the religious leaders but to his own disciples. He gave them an ominous warning: "Those who try to make their life secure will lose it, but those who lose their life will keep it" (v. 33 NRSV).

What did Jesus mean? How can you lose your life by securing it or keep your life by losing it? And what would this look like, anyway? Whatever Jesus meant, one thing was clear: this is a serious matter.

Jesus did not always use paradoxes; sometimes he taught in parables or simply interpreted the Old Testament law. At other times he just interacted in friendly conversation with people. But many of Jesus' oft-quoted teachings are paradoxes. What is it about his paradoxes that Jesus himself thought important enough to repeat again and again? And why have these paradoxes so powerfully gripped so many over time?

Jesus' paradoxes startle us by challenging our customary reasoning about life. They may initially seem nonsensical or logically inconsistent. How can we live by losing our lives? How can it help to resist evil people who hit us by turning our face to let them take another crack (Matt. 5:39)? How can a poor person gain by giving away the little she has (Luke 6:32)? Despite our initial inability to see how these kinds of statements can be true, Jesus reveals that they not only can be true, they are *essential* truths. They are powerful directives about how life really works.

The paradoxes of Jesus also grip us because they are liberating. They set us free to rejoice in life's ambiguities. I have spent time around many religious people (Christians included) and philosophers who purport to have categorical answers for everything. I have come to believe, however, that even if everything in life has an explanation, we may not have ultimate access to every explanation, at least for now. Sometimes this frustrates us, and understandably so. We like the control that we feel when we think we know all the answers. Sometimes, however, we simply cannot explain things—or at least, we cannot *adequately* explain them.

For instance, I have never felt that as a minister, or simply as a Christian, I could offer an adequate explanation—spiritual or otherwise—to a parent whose child has just died. Fumbling through my knowledge of theology or the Bible seldom helps. Paradoxically, the most helpful responses I recall are when I was so overcome with sorrow myself for the loss of the child that I wept with and embraced the grieving parent. In what way is another blubbering person a helpful response to this situation? I do not know. But oftentimes it is. Why do we have to suffer so? I do not know the answer to this either. But I do know that many survivors who have suffered tragic loss emerge healed, recounting that the loss became one of their most profound experiences of spiritual insight and personal growth.

Jesus knew that there is freedom in admitting that we do not know all the answers. At times when he could have given a clear, categorical answer to a question, he offered a paradox—a mystery statement. It seems that Jesus wanted his listeners to confess their limited nature as humans and, in the process, to acknowledge that God is the Creator and we, the created. We are liberated when we are convinced that we can do no more in a given circumstance. God is at work in powerful and positive ways behind the mystery of what we cannot explain in a given time and place.

The person who begins to learn, understand, and accept the paradoxes of Jesus becomes like the man who had been blind from birth, whom Jesus healed on a Sabbath, against then-conventional interpretations of the Jewish law (see John 9). When the blind man was hauled before a court of religious officials who demanded to know the details of the man's healing, he admitted that he didn't know how Jesus had healed him or whether Jesus had acted illegally in doing so. He simply responded, "Whether he is a sinner or not, I don't know. One thing I do know. I was blind but now I see!" (v. 25).

Some may object that rejoicing in ambiguity is a copout—an irrational glorification of what we do not understand. Not so. Like it or not, paradoxes are an integral part of reality, even if we don't understand them and even if we are not followers of Jesus. You don't need to be a Christian to acknowledge that people who are caught in the grip of materialism—who take, accumulate, and hoard—do not know the joy and freedom experienced by generous people who give without reservation. Those who require others to fit their mold before they will love them can

PARADOXY

never experience the release of loving others unconditionally and with total abandon.

Those who truly follow Jesus' teachings readily confess that they understand life differently than much of the world. A. W. Tozer once remarked,

> A real Christian is an odd number. . . . He feels supreme love for one whom he has never seen . . . empties himself in order to be full, admits he is wrong so he can be declared right . . . is strongest when he is weakest, [and is] richest when he is poorest. . . . He dies so he can live, forsakes in order to have, gives away so he can keep, sees the invisible, hears the inaudible, and knows that which surpasses knowledge.[2]

We cannot escape the realities of these paradoxes by simply denying them or by accusing those who choose to live by them of naïveté. It is better—we are better—when we embrace them as part of our daily practice.

Many of the world's philosophers and religious leaders (including Buddha, Confucius, and modern Western philosophers) taught truth by pointing to life's paradoxes, and sometimes Jesus used paradoxes in ways similar to these thinkers. But the teachings of Jesus ultimately point to much more than an ethical way of life or a novel way of viewing the world. His teachings ultimately point to himself.

Jesus laid claim to being the Anointed One, the Messiah, whom Israel had long awaited. Jesus identified himself as one with God. He told his disciples things like "I am the light of the world," "I am the bread of life," and "I am the door. If anyone enters by Me, he will be saved" (John 8:12; 6:35; 10:9 NKJV). Unlike other philosophers and religious teachers who were concerned mainly with giving new directions for human behavior, Jesus also wanted to show people how they could undergo a complete inward transformation. Jesus taught that we do this by linking our lives not merely with his teachings but with him. He calls those who have ears to hear him to listen and connect their lives to him.

Peace Redefined

The effort to learn and live out Jesus' paradoxes leads to that treasured but slippery state of personal peace. Jesus promised rest for the soul, a unique divine peace, abundant life; and he called his followers to lives without worry and concern. All of his original disciples, save John, went to martyrs' deaths attesting that he had delivered on that promise.

This quiet calm of the heart and mind that we long for is not naive blindness to the realities of life. It is an assurance that regardless of circumstances, God is with us in the midst of it all—and therefore, one way or another, we are going to be all right. This kind of peace brings a satisfaction that leaves us wonderfully emptied, longing for more of God's presence and power. Ironically, true personal peace does not come from having more of what we think we need—money, relationships, health, sexual fulfillment, career satisfaction. Sometimes the most peaceful people have very little but are the most grateful for what they do have.

The paradoxes of Jesus help us find those deep qualities of peace that we crave. But beware: we are often impatient in our desire to acquire it quickly and easily. St. Paul tells us that he had come to know the peace of Christ only by a lifelong process of practicing the paradoxical ways of Jesus—rejoicing during suffering, being prayerful and thankful in anxious times, and

PARADOXY

disciplining his mind to think on things that are noble (see Phil. 4:4–9). And while the peace he had attained surely lifted his emotions at times and brought him success as we might typically define it, Paul's peace from Christ was much more than a good mood or high achievement.

Practicing Jesus' paradoxes redefines for us the very meaning of peace. That kind of change of heart, mind, and soul is reflected in the prayer of an unknown Confederate soldier:

> I asked for strength that I might achieve;
> I was made weak that I might learn humbly to obey.
>
> I asked for health that I might do greater things;
> I was given infirmity that I might do better things.
>
> I asked for riches that I might be happy;
> I was given poverty that I might be wise.
>
> I asked for power that I might have the praise of men;
> I was given weakness that I might feel the need of God.
>
> I asked for all things that I might enjoy life;
> I was given life that I might enjoy all things.
>
> I got nothing that I asked for,
> But everything that I had hoped for.
>
> Almost despite myself my unspoken prayers were answered;
> I am, among all men, most richly blessed.[3]

The peace of Jesus is not just another modern-day narcotic. His teachings go deeper, piercing to our heart's true longings.

PEACE FOR RESTLESS SOULS

They offer spiritual insight, gratification, inner peace, personal freedom, wisdom, spiritual and moral strength, victorious confidence, a sense of true greatness, and liberating forgiveness for all who will listen and follow him.

Finding rest in Jesus is radically different from complacency or lack of ambition. St. Paul became a leader whose work honeycombed the Western world with life-giving, purpose-filled churches. He defied a government whose leaders had ruthlessly brutalized its subjects. Although Paul preached gentleness and humility, he aggressively fought for personal human dignity, political order, and the humane treatment of all.

Many who have followed the teachings of Jesus have developed lives of powerful positive influence: Augustine, Teresa of Avila, Thomas Aquinas, Desiderius Erasmus, Martin Luther, Johann Sebastian Bach, Søren Kierkegaard, Abraham Lincoln, Dietrich Bonhoeffer, C. S. Lewis, Albert Schweitzer, Mother Teresa, Martin Luther King Jr., and countless others. Becoming great was not the goal pursued by these leaders. Rather, they became great along the way by being preoccupied with other passions: they burned with passions for brutal honesty, spiritual ecstasy, brilliant thoughts, an awe for humanity, spiritual integrity, exquisite music, plunging commitment, freedom from slavery, and the exposure of injustice. Instead of seeking personal accolades, they longed to make the complex simple, heal the sick, enrich the impoverished, and bring justice for all.

Jesus' paradoxes are not just for intellectuals or the holy; they are for anyone willing to follow them. Jesus taught on hillsides and in homes, to crowds of commoners and clergy. He did not reserve his teaching exclusively for synagogues or seminaries. His teachings were for beggars and aristocrats, prostitutes and patriarchs, friends and enemies. Jesus exposed the mysteries of life's paradoxes to political sovereigns and shackled slaves. His paradoxes are not so much hard to understand as they are hard to live out—particularly until we admit that our outlook on the world is radically different from God's. But for those who earnestly seek more out of life than what they have achieved on their own, learning and practicing the paradoxes of Jesus is like being carried to the crest of a mountain and seeing the view of all that we've been missing in the valleys below.

The Path of Paradox

Our world suffers from fundamental problems with evil. The human race often sabotages its own efforts to find joy and fulfillment. We injure one another physically, emotionally, financially, and spiritually. And we are all guilty in some measure. After all, who of us can honestly say that we have never lied or cheated, that we have never been selfish or treacherous? Who of us can say that we always rise to assist the helpless and the oppressed, that we have never needed to forgive or be forgiven? Wrongdoing is the one reality that levels us all. At one time or another and in some way or other, we all conspire to commit self-destruction. Jesus' paradoxes show us that he did not ignore these realities. Instead, he taught boldly in the face of them.

The result of Jesus' boldness in confronting human evil is that we have the chance to come face-to-face with the bittersweet paradox of God's love and our failures. Facing who we are also brings real freedom and hope for renewed life.

I met a man named Don once in an alley in a barrio section of my hometown. At that time I had recently become a Christian; in idealistic but sincere passion I decided to use my time outside of high school to work in one of the poorest areas of my city, where prostitution, drunkenness, violence, and the hardest of living were all done out in the open. My parents were worried and at the same time oddly encouraged by my newfound compassion.

Don was crouched against a wall outside the back of a bar and pool hall where I often went to help people. He was about sixty-five, gray, dirty, evidently homeless. It was late at night and I was about to go home. As I passed Don, I could tell he was not just another street drunk huddled in for the night. He was injured. He winced in pain and held his arm. I knelt next to him and gently touched his very swollen forearm. He told me a night watchman had broken it in an attempt to jerk him up so that he wouldn't sleep in the alley for the night.

I took Don to the hospital. As we sat in the waiting room, we talked about God, life, his past, and hope. I listened with riveted interest as he told me with nostalgia and regret about his remarkable roller-coaster life in sports and business that eventually ended in heartache and self-imposed ruin. He showed me old tattered photographs from his wallet of his now-estranged family standing in front of formerly owned homes and assets.

I talked to Don with a passion that comes best to those who have recently experienced God's liberation, telling him how I had found Jesus Christ as a real hope for new life. He listened cautiously but longingly for something that might give him another chance. The nurse called Don in, and a doctor tended his pain and put his arm in a cast.

I took him out to get something to eat before finding him a motel for the night. As we ate, I asked him if he'd like to pray and maybe start his own journey in knowing Jesus Christ. He said yes, he would. After we prayed, we talked and ate a little more. But sadness came over Don. I asked him why, and he responded,

"I'm so glad to know God's hope. But I'm so sad that I've wasted the prime of my life."

For many who will follow Jesus' teachings, the path to peace will be paved with mixed emotions, just as Don's was. Our new-found contentment in God often comes with the awareness of what we've squandered or lost in our pasts. When we embrace God's new hope, we also comprehend painful truths about ourselves.

But strangely, acceptance of those facts brings relief. Better to live in the reality of what is than to pretend that ignorance is bliss. Confronting the brutal truth of who we are helps us to see what's so amazing about God's grace and love. Then we can begin to mend damage that we've done or experience healing that we've long needed. We find peace because we know we're accepted for who we are, not for who we could have been, and we have the hope of becoming better despite the past.

Jesus' paradoxes speak to our realities. We can find profound and consistent joy, fulfillment, and forgiveness—even in life's most difficult struggles or greatest poverty. Jesus recognized what we want but prescribed what we need. Heeding his teachings can heal our lives in ways that both gratify and cleanse us.

Jesus' way is a path of paradox—a path that will lead us to the most unlikely places to find peace with ourselves and peace with God.

2: Take a Load Off Me
Labor to Rest

Come to me, all you who are weary and burdened, and I will give you rest. Take my yoke upon you, . . . and you will find rest for your souls. For my yoke is easy and my burden is light.

Jesus

Lie down and listen to the crabgrass grow, the faucet leak, and learn to leave them so.

Marya Mannes (1904–1990)

From a third-story open window high atop a noisy, bustling street, I looked down from my modest hotel room in Bombay, India, to an intersection that was dusty from engine exhaust and dirt.[1] Like all of the endless miles of streets in Bombay, beleaguered people from the various levels of India's society crowded their way to their destination. Sick and disabled beggars squatted on the sidewalks, pawing with twisted limbs at wealthier passersby in hopes of handouts. Businesspeople occasionally offered a few rupees. Most walked by purposefully, staring straight ahead, brushing off the advances of the poor. Frazzled office workers wove their way to their exhausting but coveted clerical positions.

And then there were those who sold small goods or services on the streets. In some ways their lives seem the most difficult. They neither own businesses nor have skills for particular trades. They number in the millions, comprising much of India's population. Many such people support large extended families by selling trinkets at makeshift stands or shining shoes for what amounted to a few cents per job.

I sat and watched this swarm of humanity until a man and a little boy caught my eye. The man was gaunt and dressed in a tattered but clean white shirt and tan pants. His hair was neat, but his shoes were worn through, exposing parts of his feet. He labored to carry himself with a certain dignity as he walked to the street corner and pulled a small rolled cloth from his pants pocket. The boy, about six years old, knelt next to him as they spread the cloth on the sidewalk and placed a few shiny trinkets on the material. They seemed focused and eager to sell their wares.

That image stayed with me as I left the hotel to go about my own business for the day. When I returned around six o'clock in the evening, the street was quieter. Fewer pedestrians whisked up and down the sidewalks. But the man and the little boy were still there, displaying what appeared to be the same trinkets I had seen that morning. Preparing to leave for dinner, I wondered why they hadn't given up by now.

I returned after dark to an intersection that was all but empty, lit by two halogen street lamps. A man who had been selling large bolts of cloth was asleep on top of his parked cart. Another sipped a cup of tea in front of a small café. Then I noticed the man and the boy with the trinkets, still kneeling on the sidewalk. I watched them for a few minutes as they said a few words to each other. The man rolled up the cloth and returned it to his pants pocket. The two rose to their feet. The man's narrow shoulders hung as he looked up the street in one direction, then the other, and walked to a cement bench and sat down. The little boy dutifully followed and took his place beside him. His elbows on his knees, the man stared at the ground for a moment before he lifted his hands to wipe tears from his eyes. Seeing this, the boy gently reached up to put his arm around the troubled man's shoulder, holding it there fast while the man cried.

I jumped up to leave my room, to see if I could speak to them, to help in some way. I walked quickly down the dim hall of the building and rang a bell to call for the rickety elevator to take me on the slow descent to the lobby. When I arrived outside, I looked in all directions. They were gone. Standing alone in the middle of the street, I wished I had come down sooner. I wished I had been able to give them something to show for their efforts that day. I wished I had known them.

This scene has become a photograph in my memory that exemplifies human weariness. Not the kind of weariness that comes from running a marathon or taking a difficult exam. No. The weariness I saw in that man was the exhaustion of a life without breaks—a weariness that comes from failing despite your best efforts to provide for those who depend on you. It was a fatigue leading to a disillusionment that was vivid enough to move a little child to deep compassion. It was a weariness that millions experience—a weariness that wrings one's nerves to despair and makes a person ask, "*Now* where do I turn?" It was the kind of weariness that moved Jesus to invite people like the man with the trinkets to "come to me, all you who are weary and burdened, and I will give you rest" (Matt. 11:28).

Jesus recognized intense human weariness as a primary enemy of human peace and contentment; it is a close cousin to worry. Many of the burdens of life that grind us down also affected the people of Jesus' day. Like us, Jesus' audience worried about where to invest their life earnings. They worried about having major health problems or being audited by the "IRS" or having to speak in public. Archaeological artifacts like mirrors, combs, brushes, and makeup kits reveal that they were concerned with their appearances, as we are.

Despite modern conveniences that are intended to simplify life, our gadgets seem to bring new layers of anxiety. We worry about whether our credit card will be declined in public, whether the computer is going to work right, and whether the electric bill is going to break us this month.

As if the daily anxieties that confront us are not enough, life's rush increases our weariness as it constantly reminds us of our failings. The philosopher Eric Hoffer wrote, "Men weary as much of *not* doing the things they want to do as of doing the things they do not want to do."[2]

If anxiety is the first cause of our weariness, aimlessness follows close behind. We often lack a sense of purpose. Human life is divided into stages of development. Childhood, adolescence, teen years, and early adulthood mark the first half of our lives. Then we move into that broad second half of our lives, begin-

PARADOXY

ning anywhere from age thirty to fifty. While the first part of life is filled with learning and earning, adulthood past middle age seems in some ways more perilous. We realize that many of the dreams that we've had since our youth may not be fulfilled. When we do manage to fulfill a dream, we discover it was not all it was cracked up to be. The things that really matter come into sharper focus as we become far more aware that our time is limited.

I remember looking into my own father's pale, drawn face as he sat on an airplane just before takeoff. At seventy-one he had fallen prey to a terminal illness. He gently said to me, "You're a good son. You're a lot of fun." Everything about that moment said he wished he had the energy to stay with me longer, to get to know my two boys, his grandsons. But disease would steal that from him. His health was rapidly failing, and that statement would be the last he ever spoke to me. He died two days later.

We must live beyond the instant. We must *plan* to do those things that we think really matter—those things that we want to leave as a legacy to loved ones and the world. We must purposefully act on those things we have always wanted to experience. For some, this will bring great fulfillment.

For many, however, the frustration of unforeseen roadblocks that stand in the way of our goals drains us to exhaustion. With every passing day of expending our energy, we often realize that what we had thought would fulfill us was not really a worthy goal. Our frustration, exhaustion, and dimming energy lead us to debilitating burnout. Because of this, Jesus took precise aim at how we could best find peace, fulfillment, and rest from the burdens that bring us down.

Taking On More Burdens?

It may seem strange that Jesus did not direct those who are weary simply to take a rest or to indulge in a well-deserved break. Instead, he ironically used language that appears to encourage taking on a greater load. He told those who would follow him,

> Come to me, all you who are weary and burdened, and I will give you rest. Take my yoke upon you and learn from me, for I am gentle and humble in heart, and you will find rest for your souls. For my yoke is easy and my burden is light.
>
> Matthew 11:28–30

Much of the appeal of Jesus' statement was that he recognized the weariness that humans suffer. He did not begin with a harsh, "Buck up! Deal with it! Whatever your problem is, get over it!" He recognized that human fatigue is central and very real.

The remedy Jesus offered is a paradox: "Take my yoke upon you and learn from me." A yoke was a coupling, a wooden frame placed on the backs of draft animals to make them pull in tandem. The simple yokes consisted of a bar with two loops either of rope or wood that typically fit across the necks of work animals like oxen or mules. Jesus' language signifies servitude. Putting on his yoke means becoming his disciple, sharing in his work.

Discipleship requires a deliberate decision, action, and commitment to Jesus. Before immigrants become citizens of the United States, they must renounce all commitments and allegiances to former homelands and pledge 100 percent allegiance to America. Then and only then will the U.S. government grant them citizenship. This type of commitment is what Jesus required of those who wanted to follow.

PARADOXY

In 1986 Mother Teresa heard vows from eleven new members of her growing order, the *Society of the Missionaries of Charity*. Afterward she commented, "Love, to be real, must cost. It must hurt. It must empty us of self."[3]

Similarly, Jesus tells us to learn from him, discipleship style, by following him. This means not merely listening to Jesus' words but also following his way of life—making his preoccupations our preoccupations. The teachings that motivated him should motivate us. The experiences that broke Jesus' heart should break ours. And what broke Jesus' heart? People in the greatest kind of need. Hopeless people without advocates or a personal relationship with God.

In the New Testament book of Luke, the author records Jesus' lamenting how widely people missed God's good plans for them. It reads, "As he approached Jerusalem and saw the city, he wept over it and said, 'If you, even you, had only known on this day what would bring you peace—but now it is hidden from your eyes'" (Luke 19:41–42). What broke Jesus' heart was that they misunderstood *him*—the incarnation of God's peace. But peace comes at a cost.

Jesus' call to discipleship was that his followers would exchange their burdens for his, and part of what it meant to take on Jesus' yoke was to learn from him. In his book *The Rise and Fall of the Third Reich*, William L. Shirer says that during the Nazi regime, Hitler recognized how important it was to control the schools.[4] The German schools, from first grade through the universities, were quickly "Nazified." In a speech on November 6, 1933, Hitler said,

> When an opponent declares, "I will not come over to your side," I calmly say, "Your child belongs to us already. . . ." What are you?

TAKE A LOAD OFF ME

You will pass on. Your descendants, however, now stand in the new camp. In a short time they will know nothing else but this new community.[5]

Hitler later declared on May 1, 1937, "This new Reich will give its youth to no one, but will itself take youth and give to youth its own education and its own upbringing."[6] In other words, those who control the classroom often control the future.

The same premise espoused by Hitler also applies to learning in general. What we learn—what we read, watch on television, view on the Internet, or hear from our friends or teachers—shapes us and all that we become. And what we become determines whether we have enough stamina to endure life's struggles. What we have allowed to form our character determines the degree to which we will withstand our most difficult life challenges.

Jesus' statement is a word of caution as much as it is an invitation. "Follow *me*," Jesus once told several of his closest disciples. This meant "follow *me*, as opposed to all of the other voices who call you to follow *them*." The worthiness and credibility of the voice that we follow matter enormously. Why? Because following the right voice is our only assurance that we will reach our desired destinations emotionally, spiritually, physically, and relationally intact. It's that assurance that gives us rest.

The Promise of Accepting Jesus' Yoke

Finally, Jesus promises two things for those who take on his kind of burden. First, he promises lasting peace and rest. He says, "Take my yoke upon you . . . , for I am gentle and humble in heart, and you will find rest for your souls" (Matt. 11:29). Ancient

PARADOXY

mariners have long told that in stormy weather it is not unusual for small birds to be blown out to sea, far away from land. They hover over ships' masts, desperately in need of rest but afraid to land. A story is told of one such bird that, in utter exhaustion, landed on a traveler's ship after following it for a considerable distance.[7] The little bird was so worn-out that the traveler easily caught it, and it nestled its cold feet into its feathers, resting in the warmth of the man's hand. The traveler said that the bird looked around in the pleasantness of his hand, not the least bit afraid. It had lighted with one whom it could trust.

Like the little bird, we too find ourselves blown out to seas of moral and spiritual disorientation and despair. Jesus Christ extends a warm reception to us, welcoming any exhausted pilgrim who commits his or her life into Jesus' hands. We all need that kind of rest. The New Testament Gospels recount that Jesus himself frequently left the crowds that followed him and took time to rest either in solitude or with his closest friends.

The Greeks had a saying: "You will break the bow if you keep it always bent." Many of us know all too well the price we pay for our workaholism. We think it demonstrates to others that we are industrious, hardworking, responsible people. But all too often, it is only a mask for our inability to be alone with ourselves, God, and others close to us. Too often, workaholism merely reflects how empty and indefinable our lives are outside of what we do or the possessions we have.

We somehow think that if we avoid solitude and silence, keep up the pace, and continue our chatter, our noise will block God's penetrating presence. The silence reveals how vacuous our lives really are. Yet it is perhaps most often in peaceful and quiet solitude that we find not only the wise judgment of God but also his loving peace. The Old Testament, which Jesus knew and regularly recited, says, "Be still and know that I am God" (Ps. 46:10). "Take my yoke upon you," Jesus invited, ". . . and you will find rest for your souls."

Lightening Your Load . . . with a New One

The second thing that Jesus promises those who take on his yoke is that they will experience a new lightness of being. He concluded his teaching on rest for the weary with the greatest irony of all: "Take my yoke upon you...for my yoke is easy and my burden is light" (Matt. 11:29–30). But how can a burden be light? How can a yoke of servitude, even to Jesus, result in an easiness and lightness in living that we cannot experience while serving our own desires and interests? Jesus is calling us to the kind of relationship that God designed us to have with him. The letter to the church at Ephesus in the New Testament puts it this way: "For we are God's workmanship, created in Christ Jesus to do good works, which God prepared in advance for us to do" (Eph. 2:10).

We are most contented when our lives purposefully serve God and others. God's love empowers in us a zest for life, which overcomes the aimlessness that drives us to exhaustion. We see glimpses of this when we experience relationships of deep love with others.

No experience has changed me more joyously than becoming a father. When my wife, Jan, was pregnant with our first child, Aaron, she had to remain in the hospital the final week of her pregnancy because of high blood pressure. During that week, I not only had to maintain commitments at my job, I also faced a deadline to finish my first book and needed to remodel a room

PARADOXY

in our house that would be Aaron's new nursery. I worked at my job all day, then came home and wrote for several hours. Usually beginning after midnight, I worked to remodel Aaron's room.

I vividly recall that those late-night hours were the joy of my day. Despite the lack of sleep, the paint fumes, the dirt, the dust, and the sweat, working on that room was like having an incredible dessert after a bland meal. Nothing made me happier than rolling up my sleeves and creating Aaron's new space. I knew that the day was coming when I would bring that little boy home in my arms, place him in his new crib, and say, "Welcome to your home. Relax, because here you are loved beyond your wildest dreams." My work in that nursery was not like work at all. I expended energy but gladly came back for more the next night until the job was done. It was a labor of love. And it is this kind of servitude that brings us the satisfaction we long for.

If we truly commit to Jesus, we soon see that we have committed not to another heavy burden but to the greatest labor of love. We have committed to a life worth living, with ends worth attaining, for a Master worth serving.

Compare this kind of commitment to the kind found in jobs that you tolerate or even despise. Taking up the calling of Jesus Christ to rest from weariness and be his disciple is to do something that one would do with pleasure. It is comparable to creating something in fervent anticipation of giving it to a loved one—something that might give a child a better future or that might pay off another's debt whom you want to see set free from the burden.

The difference is that the rest, peace, and freedom attained will be *yours*. We win in the end, not because of what we have somehow done for God, but because we place our trust and confidence in God who is indeed able to give us those gifts.

TAKE A LOAD OFF ME

A true discipleship commitment to Jesus Christ does not drain us but gives our lives vitality and refreshment. It regenerates and nourishes us to be able to press on through all that might assail us. In John 7:37–38 Jesus said, "Let anyone who is thirsty come to me, and let the one who believes in me drink" (NRSV). Or as Jesus also said, "Out of the believer's heart shall flow rivers of living water" (v. 39 NRSV). Committed discipleship quenches the thirst that otherwise wearies the undirected life. Jesus' lordship and leadership heals our weariness by giving us purpose rather than aimlessness. We no longer need to pull ourselves up by our own bootstraps or find our own way out of our predicaments. God dispenses with these self-imposed and impotent requirements. Instead, he empowers us by the indwelling of the very Spirit of God to imagine and create new possibilities for hopeful, vibrant futures.

Rest for the Weary

According to Jesus, finding the rest that we seek from the weariness of life requires us to do at least three things. First, we must commit our lives in discipleship to him. We do this through consistent prayer. When we are persistent with God, we place ourselves spiritually in the restful presence of God, no matter where we are physically, mentally, or emotionally. The New Testament book of Revelation quotes Jesus saying, "Here I am! I stand at the door and knock. If anyone hears my voice and opens the door, I will come in and eat with him, and he with me" (3:20). This is a picture of Jesus Christ wanting to have steady companionship with us.

For many, this step of discipleship makes them bristle. They presume that it means one must give up all enjoyments of life.

PARADOXY

But this is misguided. Indeed, giving up those things that have led us to lives of empty exhaustion makes perfect sense. We give up little by comparison of what we gain in Jesus Christ. A famous missionary of the 1950s, Jim Elliot, recast Jesus' call for disciples this way: "He is no fool who gives what he cannot keep to gain what he cannot lose." Those who have experienced Jesus Christ's power to soothe them after knowing the hammering fatigue as described in Matthew 11 realize which is clearly the better end of the trade.

Second, we must trust Christ as the source of rest from our weariness. Pastor Dietrich Bonhoeffer, who was imprisoned and hanged for refusing to submit to the demands of the Nazi regime, wrote in his book *The Cost of Discipleship*:

> If we answer the call to discipleship, where will it lead us? What decisions and partings will it demand? To answer this question we shall have to go to Him, for only He knows the answer. Only Jesus Christ who bids us follow Him, knows the journey's end. But we do know that it will be a road of boundless mercy. Discipleship means joy.[8]

For most of us, it's hard to trust people in very deep ways. We're always afraid they want some advantage over us. Coworkers might use our vulnerabilities as a means to outshine us. Family members might use our deepest confidences to hurt or criticize us. And God only knows what some stranger may do if we trust them with our lives. Yet trust is exactly what Jesus asks for. It's the only means that he offers for us to really know his rest and peace. He calls us to tell him our most private thoughts and secrets—the things that we are proud of as well as ashamed of. Then he promises to handle them with tender grace and mercy like no one else will.

Finally, we must slow down. Jesus spoke strongly and frequently about the topic of worry, saying things like, "Do not worry about tomorrow, for tomorrow will worry about itself. Each day has enough trouble of its own" (Matt. 6:34). This is no mean thing for many. All too often we subsist on worry, which in turn depletes our energy. We are like the drug addict who lives from day to day, from fix to frenzied, unfulfilling fix.

Yet Jesus bids you and me to stop living this way. He invites us to come to him in the solitude of prayer. Dare to step away from your schedule, your work, your friends. Ask him to quiet those screaming demands that have left your life in unrest. Have confidence that Jesus Christ has the power and desire to melt away the chains of weariness that entangle you.

Meditation

> Lord Jesus, make my heart sit down.
>
> African proverb[9]

3: When Seeing Isn't Believing

Walk by Faith, Not by Sight

Do you have eyes but fail to see?

Jesus

Faith is the vision of the heart; it sees God in the dark as well as in the day.

Author Unknown

Scott roomed across the hall from me during my first year at a small Christian college in the Midwest. He was strikingly different from other students for a number of reasons. He came from a severely conservative religious background. His clothes were glaringly dated—usually a white short-sleeve shirt, a thin black tie, and dark pants. He wore thick black glasses and had his hair buzzed to stubble, exposing white sidewalls. This was the late seventies, so Scott's look would not return as a fashion statement until the *Revenge of the Nerds* movie series hit theaters a decade later.

But more than his dress, two things made Scott stand out from other students. First, he was blind, or nearly so. He was in the final stages of glaucoma, which had begun some years earlier and had progressed to almost complete loss of sight. During classes he'd fumble with a tape recorder so later he could listen to professors' lectures. He'd awkwardly find his way down the hall to go to the showers or classes in the mornings. I would love to say I admired Scott, but I didn't. In fact, few did. This was because of Scott's final distinguishing characteristic: his arrogance. In the few instances when he interacted with the rest of us, Scott spoke with an obnoxious tone of religious superiority and self-righteousness. No matter what the topic of conversation, Scott smirked or snorted, implying his disdain for the ideas of others and his presumption that he had the truly spiritual read on all life's issues.

Scott was a real puzzle. You wanted at least to feel sorry for the guy, yet he somehow defied everyone's pity. He was a bewildering balance between the insufferable and the ill fated, and yet he seemed oblivious to both.

Despite Scott's somewhat grating style, I liked him. Beneath his arrogance was a guy who was really very bright and who wanted to be normal. His brashness also revealed a brutal honesty toward others that I envied. I was pretty sure that, like all of us, he wanted to be liked, not pitied.

I wanted to befriend him, but I also wanted to tell him that he was often unbearable. In the midst of my quandary, our circumstances started to resolve themselves. In those early weeks at school before we had gotten to know many people, many of

PARADOXY

the students would go out to have fun on Friday and Saturday nights. But Scott and I were still staying in our rooms. He would always leave his room door open, and I'd wander over to his room to try to make conversation. But his responses were so terse, so off-putting, that I would return to my room stymied about how to respond.

One Friday night I went over to talk to Scott as he sat alone in his room. I don't remember the topic, but I do remember Scott starting in with his typical responses. It set me off. "You know what?" I said, "You're a jerk." He recoiled, but instead of reacting angrily, he asked with an embarrassed nervousness, "What do you mean?"

I calmed down and began to tell him what people thought of him. To my surprise, he listened. He drank in my words with a humility that made me assess my own shortcomings. Our talk was the beginning of a friendship. Over that next year I saw Scott open up and become a regular person. He appreciated the opinions of other people. He laughed as people teased him about his time-warped wardrobe. He saw his own pretense, and in humble and effective ways, he helped me see some of my pretense too.

The most interesting thing about Scott I learned that year, however, was what had driven his spiritual blindness. It was fear. Scott was afraid of losing his sight, of what it might mean for him later in life when he was no longer with his parents or in a dormitory. Scott left college for a year to enter a program sponsored by the National Federation for the Blind—a program designed to acclimate those with limited or lost vision to live alone and in mainstream society.

Scott and I corresponded via letters and cassette tapes for a few years. One of the most gratifying experiences of my life came when I listened to a tape he sent: he was not only graduating, he

WHEN SEEING ISN'T BELIEVING

was marrying a wonderful woman, and he had become a vice president for the National Federation of the Blind. Scott's words were incredibly encouraging about how much our friendship had meant to him. His friendship meant a lot to me too. In addition to showing me some of my faults, Scott taught me the value of taking the time to engage with people who initially seem difficult.

Humanity suffers from spiritual blindness—the inability or unwillingness to believe. It's the impediment that prevents us from seeing what matters most in this life. Jesus' three-year earthly ministry demonstrated that some of the blindest are the religious. Healing all of us and giving us real spiritual insight has been one of Jesus' most important missions.

Finding Insight as Better Sight

I don't think I have ever known anyone who expressly said he or she wanted to bumble through life randomly. At one time or another, all of us may live aimlessly. But most want to live purposefully, based on *insight* into those things that really matter. In fact, we spend a good deal of time, money, and effort trying to figure out what will give our lives purpose and meaning.

Insight is strongly analogous to physical sight. When we grope about in a dark, unfamiliar room, we feel shapes and may even know what they are. Yet, often we do not know how the shapes stand in relation to one another. In the dark we do not know how to navigate the room. We need light to help us find the way.

Without insight, we stumble through life, ignorant and unaware of how to read people and circumstances. Insight helps us understand life in context and tells us how facts stand in relation to one another. Insight helps us navigate life.

Jesus' Teachings about Faith as True Insight

The faith Jesus taught about is a kind of insight. Many misunderstand faith to be otherworldly or abstract. But faith, as Jesus referred to it, lays out the true ground rules of life; faith is intensely practical. It is a way of viewing our world as it *really* is, and not in merely physical, superficial terms. Faith is seeing life as God sees it.

Understanding faith intellectually is not enough. Jesus taught that faith is effective only if we embrace and experience it personally. Most of us have difficulty attaining and maintaining lives of faith. We are easily distracted by desires for and attachments to people, material things, or selfish demands. But when we develop a healthy life of insight brought about by faith, we find a newness of life free of obsessive attachments.

The Problem with Faith

The gospel of Mark reports a time when Jesus was frustrated with his disciples. They had already spent considerable time with Jesus, seeing him perform miracles and hearing many of his teachings on spiritual insight. Still, his disciples complained when they realized they had not brought enough bread along in their boat for everyone to eat. Jesus was frustrated with their lack of confidence in him and with their failure to understand his power to provide for them. "Why are you talking about having no bread? Do you still not perceive or understand? Are your hearts hardened? Do you have eyes, and fail to see?" (Mark 8:17–18 NRSV).

Jesus equates a lack of spiritual insight with a "hardened heart"—a common biblical reference to one's refusal to view life in a new way. This almost seems harsh. After all, the disciples were only concerned that everyone in their boat had enough food for the trip. But Jesus' strong interrogation was warranted and ultimately effective.

Jesus rebuked his disciples because they had just seen Jesus feed an audience of over five thousand people with a few loaves of bread and two fish (see Mark 6:30–44). They had heard his countless teachings about how they should not worry because God would meet their daily needs. The disciples certainly purported to have lives of faith; otherwise, they would not have followed Jesus or any other religious teacher as disciples. When Jesus questioned his disciples' commitment to him, they became indignant that he would even suggest that they were less than totally committed. Clearly, the disciples held themselves out as spiritual people.

Despite all this, they failed to trust him. They had not simply forgotten all that should make them trust Jesus' power and kindness. Jesus was angry because they *refused* to see their own lives through God's new possibilities. Jesus reprimanded his disciples because they, of all people, refused to recognize what it means to trust God. And so, throughout the Gospels, Jesus repeatedly rebukes his own disciples as "people of little faith."

O We of Little Faith

Jesus' earthly ministry with his disciples lasted for about three years. During that time, his disciples followed him with reservations and partial awareness of his true identity and power. Their faith wavered regularly. At times they seemed more curious about Jesus than committed to him. The disciples were inconsistent at best.

PARADOXY

We should not, however, look disdainfully on these first-century followers. Most of us who claim to follow Jesus share their tendencies. We fade in and out of our beliefs and commitments. Anyone who is honest about his or her faith is likely to be at least occasionally convicted by Jesus' indictments of his disciples.

No matter how often we see God's deliverance and guidance, we still doubt and sometimes even deny God's existence or presence. Just like the disciples, we sometimes pretend to maintain spiritual insight even when inwardly we are wavering. We, like the disciples, fail to fess up. We live as if everything is okay. We speak the language of faith without our hearts comprehending it.

I saw a vivid analogy of this several years ago when I traveled to Germany with my wife, Jan. Ten years prior, I had studied and traveled in Germany for nearly a year. I learned to speak German with modest fluency while living with the family Jan and I were now visiting. When we entered their house, Jan and the mother of the family, Ms. Janssen, approached each other. Jan speaks no German and Ms. Janssen speaks no English. Believing, as most of us do when we don't actually speak a language, that they could understand one another by making gestures and speaking loudly, they began to converse, or so they thought. As they each spoke in their respective languages, I understood both of them, and I listened to their rapidly deteriorating conversation.

Ms. Janssen said, "Did you have a good trip? It is so nice to finally meet you."

Jan responded, "We had a nice trip here. It's wonderful to meet you."

"You must be hungry. Can I get you something to eat? How about some grapes?" asked Ms. Janssen.

"No, we first flew to Munich and then drove here," said my wife. "But we got to see a number of pretty sights on the way."

"Okay then, sit here at the table and I'll get you a bowlful, along with some coffee and cake," said Ms. Janssen.

And so continued their alleged conversation, as I listened on the sidelines, thinking, "Am I in the same universe here?"

We can't force something to make sense just by thinking it does or willing it into reality. To truly understand a language, we must learn and practice it. Similarly, a person who acknowledges the spiritual underpinnings of life has to learn the grammar, ways, and world of faith. According to Jesus, we learn about faith paradoxically, by trusting not what we see but what we cannot see.

Seeing Is Not Always Believing

We moderns are deeply enamored with science. This is understandable since its advancements benefit us daily. But our adulation of science leads many to skepticism about God and spiritual realities. Modern science is based on the presumption that certainty and understanding of objects and events are best attained by observation via the senses (i.e., through sight, touch, hearing, smell, and taste). After the first human space flight in April 12, 1961, Soviet cosmonaut Yuri Gagarin was quoted as saying, "I don't see any god up here." Many presume, "If I cannot see, hear, feel, or otherwise physically sense God, God must not exist." But consider the flaws in this thinking.

First, science voluntarily limits what it intends to explain from the outset when it focuses exclusively on what is physically verifiable. Science can tell us whether a fetus is in a mother's womb, but it cannot tell us if the fetus is a *person*. Science is based

PARADOXY

on assumptions that are intended to offer only certain kinds of explanations. Let's imagine I said, "God is in the next room." A nonbeliever enters the room and sees two people eating together at a table. Based solely on the assumptions of science, the non-believer may well declare, "God was not in that room." But let's further imagine that a Christian goes into the same room and sees two people praying together. One of them has a small piece of bread and shares it with the other who has none. Based on what she saw and certain biblical assumptions, the Christian may well declare that God is indeed in the room (see Matt. 18:20; 25:35–45). Is the nonbeliever right? Wrong? What about the Christian? Surely the answers lie in the *kind* of explanation that one is looking for.

Second, when we determine what is real solely on the basis of our sensory experience, we ignore ways in which we regularly perceive reality. Tell a groom that his love for his bride is not real simply because he cannot offer physical proof of it. Love causes us to alter life plans; make personal sacrifices; and undergo mental, emotional, and even physical changes. Chemical and pheromonal explanations alone, for example, cannot explain how couples fall in love through letters without ever having met. We talk commonly about love, mental intent, the equator, and myriad other things as real even though we do not physically sense them. Similarly, God and spiritual things are quite reasonably viewed as real despite their elusive natures.

Finally, our senses have limitations. They can mislead, giving us imperfect or incomplete explanations of our experience. Even ancient Greek philosophers who first developed theories about how to test physical realities acknowledged this with examples; for instance, a straight oar appears bent in the water. Typically, people explain their experiences based on a combination of their sensory experiences within the context of their worldview. And so two people looking at the same thing or event often account for it in different ways.

Even if science could successfully explain all reality by means of observation, it still does not provide belief or trust in what we experience. I can see, hear, and touch, and still not trust something or someone. Belief and trust of at least some kind are necessary for human survival. Seeing is *not* necessarily believing—and believing often has nothing to do with seeing.

Believing Is Not Always Seeing

Jesus was fully aware of the human tendency to trust the senses in order to validate faith. But he discouraged that kind of limited thinking as a hindrance to the deepest kind of faith. In the New Testament book of John, chapter 20, Jesus met one of his disciples, Thomas, who doubted reports that Jesus had risen from the dead. Jesus clearly knew that Thomas needed physical verification to support his faith. But Jesus also knew that some would believe without first seeing, and he declared they would be especially blessed for it.

Doubt is not the only enemy of faith. Sheer complacency is another. Jesus taught that many would hear his teachings, see his miracles, and yet still refuse to entrust their lives to his divinity. Luke records the parable of the ungodly rich man who descends into the afterlife. He is tormented in Hades because during his life he refused to show mercy to the poor. He pleads with Abraham, whom he sees across a great chasm, to go and tell his family of the dangers of ignoring God during their lifetimes. But, Jesus reports, Abraham tells him that would be futile: "If they do not

PARADOXY

listen to Moses and the prophets, neither will they be convinced even if someone rises from the dead" (Luke 16:31 NRSV). Luke wrote his Gospel not long after Jesus had been resurrected, and many still ignored and rejected Jesus as Messiah. In the face of Jesus' resurrection, seeing did not always result in believing.

The hearts of some nonbelievers harden even when experiencing God's power and presence. Others seem to continue in their skepticism while inwardly they are being persuaded by extraordinary experiences of God. Some time ago I presided over a funeral for a man who had been a self-proclaimed skeptic about religion. He was an attorney and a fine person for whom I had great admiration. Despite his lifelong public proclamations that he was not a religious believer, at his funeral the man's family revealed he had occasionally confessed a private persuasion of the profundity of certain biblical texts and of particular experiences that pointed to the reality of God. One of the man's sons recounted a story about when the man fought in World War II.

He was advancing with troops into a town to make sure it was abandoned. The man ran into one small house to the basement stairs with a grenade in hand, ready to throw it into the cellar. He hesitated. He recalled having an overwhelming internal sense that told him, *Wait*. He stepped down a couple of stairs into the basement. Pulling back a tattered curtain at the bottom of the staircase, the man found a huddled family on their knees praying. He placed the ring back in his grenade and slowly backed up the staircase, leaving the family in peace. He never forgot the event, and neither did those who knew him best, who saw the secretive ways in which he held a belief in the Almighty.

Jesus was intent on conveying one key teaching about our reaction to experiences with the divine: Witnessing miracles is not the basis of faith in God. Rather, having faith in God is the

WHEN SEEING ISN'T BELIEVING

basis upon which one will truly see the miraculous. How did Jesus convey this principle? Often he would perform miracles and then demand that his disciples remain quiet about them. He frequently refused to perform miracles upon demand. Why? Because Jesus had a higher purpose than performing magic tricks to satisfy the voyeuristic curiosities of spectators. He expressed a fundamental distrust of those who suggested that if only they could see a miracle, they would believe.

Even when people do believe, the strength of their faith is not the source or cause of God's power. Rather, Jesus taught, God will work in the life of anyone who will simply trust God's existence, power, mercy, and righteousness rather than their own. Jesus endorsed that kind of faith as the prerequisite for those who wanted to experience God.

One woman came to Jesus with utter confidence that he could heal her lifelong physical ailment of hemorrhaging (Mark 5:25–34). Upon touching Jesus' robe, she was healed. Jesus responded, "Daughter, your *faith* has made you well; go in peace" (v. 34 NRSV, emphasis added). The woman believed and *then* experienced the miracle. Sometimes, it was the mere admission of a lack of faith that became a factor in a miracle. Jesus told the father of a sick boy that healing was possible if people had faith, and the man responded, "I believe; help my unbelief!" (Mark 9:23–24 NRSV). Jesus immediately healed his son. When a Roman officer sought Jesus to ask for the healing of his servant, Jesus responded, "'I have not found so great faith, no, not in Israel.' . . . And his servant was healed in the selfsame hour" (Matt. 8:10, 13 KJV; see also Mark 2:5).

Repeated instances like these revealed Jesus' suspicion toward those who simply came to see his miracles. It was not seeing, touching, or otherwise physically experiencing Jesus that

PARADOXY

prompted belief in what he taught. Instead, true faith preceded experience of the divine.

We Walk by Faith, Not by Sight

How will our lives change if we begin living according to Jesus' directive of accepting God's active, unseen wonders and his love for us? One person who truly came to live as though God was actively at work in all of life was the apostle Paul. In his life we can observe the changes that seeing the unseen can make in us. He talked about this in his second letter to the Christians in the ancient city of Corinth.

> So we do not lose heart . . . because we look not at what can be seen but at what cannot be seen; for what can be seen is temporary, but what cannot be seen is eternal.
> For we know that if the earthly tent we live in is destroyed, we have a building from God, a house not made with hands, eternal in the heavens. . . . So we are always confident; even though we know that . . . we are at home in the body . . . for we walk by faith, not by sight.
>
> 2 Corinthians 4:16, 18–5:1, 6–7 NRSV

A few things occur for the believer who grasps Jesus' paradox about spiritual insight. First, he or she sees life from God's perspective—that is, life as eternal and not just temporary. This powerful truth puts all of our struggles and discouragements in comforting perspective. The problems we face today are just that—*today's* problems.

On a balmy October afternoon in 1982, Badger Stadium in Madison, Wisconsin, was packed with over 60,000 University of Wisconsin fans. They were watching their football team play Michigan State's Spartans.

It soon became obvious that State had the better team and would win the game. What was odd, however, were the seemingly unconnected and increasing eruptions of applause and shouts from the Wisconsin fans despite the mounting defeat. Why were they cheering as their team was losing? It turns out that many of the fans were listening to portable radios broadcasting another game in progress seventy miles away where Wisconsin's Milwaukee Brewers were beating the St. Louis Cardinals in game three of the World Series. They were responding to something unseen, not to what they could see before them. Likewise, Paul encourages us to fix our eyes not on what is seen but on what is unseen. When we do, we celebrate even in difficulties because we are tuned in to see God's larger picture at work.[1]

Once we have committed our hearts, projects, relationships, and possessions to God, we can trust that God has a plan that transcends all that we can see as we move through life. The Old Testament prophet Jeremiah knew this. Even though he prophesied that his countrymen would fall to brutal foreign powers, he also prophesied God's enduring bright promise for his people: "For surely I know the plans I have for you, says the Lord, plans for your welfare and not for harm, to give you a future with hope" (Jer. 29:11 NRSV). God's unseen plan for us supersedes all of our circumstances. If we live with that in mind, we can experience God's power and peace even in the toughest of conditions.

In 2 Corinthians St. Paul says that the follower of Jesus can live confidently because God's promise for his future is guaranteed by the indwelling of the Holy Spirit. This does not mean that Christians live confidently only because of the promise of heaven. In fact, Paul is combating that one-sided notion. I cringe when I hear Christians

PARADOXY

speak about the spiritual life purely in otherworldly terms. I sympathize with nonbelievers who scoff at the "pie in the sky when you die" mentality of some Christians. That view ignores the larger biblical message that Paul is conveying in 2 Corinthians—God's power and presence are available to us *here and now*! Certainly, we rest in the assurance of knowing the security of our futures. But Paul presents the whole picture: whether we are in our bodies or with the Lord, we can be confident, because with God's presence indwelling us, we are at home in either place.

Finally, those who choose to live by faith and not by sight live not according to the limited parameters of what they see but by the limitless possibilities of God. In a letter to the church at the Greek city of Philippi, St. Paul wrote, "And my God will meet all your needs according to his glorious riches in Christ Jesus" (Phil. 4:19). I have reeled at how some butcher this passage to suggest that it means God wants to make us all financially rich. This trivializes Paul's point. He wrote this to a community of poor Christians who had been staggeringly generous with the little they had, sharing with other first-century Christians in need. Paul reached out in faithful encouragement, reassuring them that God could, and in their case would, meet their needs. His point seemed to be that trusting in God for our provision in times of need rather than trusting in the thickness of our wallets is precisely what brings God's care for us into sharp focus.

I have traveled to and worked in several places where people are starving or living in desperate want. In many of those places I met faithful Christians who trust God more deeply on a daily basis than do wealthy Christians in developed countries whose faith pales by comparison. In contexts like that, Paul's message in Philippians seems especially pointed, the human condition notwithstanding.

WHEN SEEING ISN'T BELIEVING

Paul, like Jesus, knew that a major malady of the human condition is worry. And worry is often precipitated by the scarcity of our resources. Obedience to Jesus' teaching that we live under the reality of God's provision for us, no matter how little we have or how God chooses to provide, is in the end the *only* real remedy for us to combat worry.

In the aftermath of Hurricane Katrina and its ensuing floods, tens of thousands of profoundly poor people who had been ravaged by that natural disaster called out to God in faith. Did they find God faithful? If by that question we mean, did God provide for them in all the ways we presume God should have or exactly as they asked him to, then no, God didn't necessarily do that. But, if by that we mean some had their prayers precisely and tangibly answered, while others found solace, comfort, and even a surprising sense of g ntefulness because God used the generosity of others to help meet needs, then yes, God did that.

Through the media, we heard how local, state, and federal governments, which were burgeoning with billions of dollars' worth of aid, had failed people or how people experienced times of genuine despair. But in radio and television interviews, articles, and anecdotes that floated around the world after that event, we heard countless stories of how people were grateful that, after emerging from a storm that took all they had, God had still spared them. We heard how people had changed their minds about what they thought really mattered the most. And we heard how God shook the nation and the world from complacent slumber and called them to open their homes, bank accounts, closets, and garages to help wherever they could.

No doubt some people felt abandoned by God. I admit that at those times, a cynical sense of panic and doubt often grips me and causes me to demand, "Okay, God, a little assist here. We've got a catastrophe happening. Where are you?!" When events like that happen, somehow I expect that sense of mistrust to be the norm in others too. Yet, it's not. Each time, to my surprise, I find that people pray. They trust God. And then they report that, to their astonishment, with changed eyes and hearts, God came through. More clearly than ever, God met their needs and met them face-to-face in their worst life-storm.

It is a cruel and erroneous interpretation of Paul's writings to say that those who have plenty trust God, and those who don't are godless. Yet people who rely most on God in severe circumstances find God faithful when they need him most.

Dealing with the problem of evil and suffering is beyond the scope of this book. But we know that as we seek God's help in our hardships, his provision sometimes comes exactly as we think it should. Sometimes it comes in ways we don't understand at first, and we ask God why. In either case, faith is the basis for our relationship with him. Faith's rival is worry—in worry we walk through life alone. It robs us of our close relationship with God, the very thing that he desires and that calms our hearts the most.

Eye Exam

Let me offer three suggestions. The first is to ask yourself, where am I today on my journey toward the kind of insight I need? Am I navigating life according to a frustrating, limited perspective or according to the limitless possibilities of God? What grand vistas *could* I dream of if I truly begin to live out my days with the reality of God's power and presence residing in me? Ask these questions to diagnose your spiritual sight.

WHEN SEEING ISN'T BELIEVING

Next, turn the focus of your thoughts and energy toward the promise of God's trustworthiness. This very act will demonstrate that you seek the unseen. To do this is to exercise the kind of faith that Jesus honored in his New Testament ministry. In a famous message that Jesus preached on a rural hillside, he promised, "Ask and it will be given to you; seek and you will find. . . . For everyone who asks receives; he who seeks finds" (Matt. 7:7–8). Whatever your situation, tell God, "I want to see what you have for me. I will trust you with my problems. I recognize that only you can take care of them. I can't; they are beyond me." Then thank God for his provisions for you.

Finally, prepare to change. One of the most surprising things about having our eyes opened to the world of God is not how the world changes but how *we* change. Henri Nouwen rightly points out that taking these steps is seldom easy. Truth be told, it can be painful, because these steps require us to let go of familiar ways, even if we aren't proud of them. You say, "I want to be different, but somehow I don't think I can." Nouwen writes:

> You still feel jealous of the fellow who is better paid than you are, you still want revenge on someone who doesn't respect you, you are still disappointed that you've received no letter, still angry because she didn't smile when you walked by. You live through it, you live along with it as though it didn't really bother you . . . until the moment that you want to pray. Then everything returns: the bitterness, the hate, the jealousy, the disappointment and the desire for revenge. But these feelings are not just there; you clutch them in your hands as if they were treasures you didn't want to part with. You sit rummaging in all that old sourness as if you couldn't do without it, as if in giving it up, you would lose your very self.[2]

Jesus invites you to escape from that kind of fatalism. Dare to rise above your history and circumstances. Turn your focus from your failures to God's faithfulness. Acknowledge the pledge of God's promise to you, and see the unseen.

Meditation

> Lord, guide me. If you try me,
>> send me out into the foggy night,
>> so that I cannot see my way.
> Even if I stumble, this I beg,
>> that I may look and smile serenely,
>> bearing witness that you are with me
>> and I walk in peace.
> If you try me, send me out into an atmosphere
>> too thin for me to breathe
>> and I cannot feel the earth beneath my feet,
> let my behavior show men that they
>> cannot part me forcibly from you
>> in whom we breathe and move and are.
> If you let hate hamper and trap me,
>> twist my heart, disfigure me,
>> then give my eyes, his love and peace,
>> my face the expression of your Son.[3]

> Dom Helder Camara, *The Desert Is Fertile*

4: Satisfaction Guaranteed
Give to Receive

It is more blessed to give than to receive.

Jesus

Blessed are those who can give without remembering, and take without forgetting.

Princess Elizabeth (Asquith) Bibesco

There is an urban legend about a Charlotte, North Carolina, man who purchased a case of very rare and outrageously expensive cigars. He immediately insured them against . . . you guessed it—fire. Within about a month he smoked all of them. Without having paid a single insurance payment, the man filed a claim against the insurance company for his "loss." The stated basis of his claim was that the cigars were lost "in a series of small fires." The insurance company refused to pay, citing the obvious reason that the man had used the cigars for their intended purpose. Undeterred, the man sued the company and won.

The judge's ruling stated that the man held a legal policy from the company, which had warranted the cigars as insurable and had contracted to insure the cigars against fire. Nowhere had the policy specified what was or was not an "insurable fire." Thus, the judge held, the company was legally obligated to compensate the man for his loss.

Rather than endure a lengthy and costly appeal process, the insurance company accepted the judge's ruling and paid the man $15,000 for the rare cigars he lost in "the fires." After the man cashed the check, however, the insurance company had him arrested . . . on twenty-four counts of arson.

Using the man's own insurance claim and testimony recorded in his previous court case as evidence against him, the man was convicted of intentionally setting fire to the rare cigars. He was sentenced to twenty-four consecutive one-year terms.

Greed Backfires

We expend astonishing amounts of energy devising ingenious—sometimes even deceitful—ways to wring every drop of worth out of what we have. But why? Why is enough rarely enough? Why are those with the most often those who demand still more? Do we presume that if we continue to get more, at some point we will magically be satisfied? Oddly, no matter how many zeros are behind the first number in our bank accounts, no matter how many experiences of pampering and luxury, and no matter what we come to possess, we find our

PARADOXY

greed growing rather than shrinking when we feed it. And rather than satisfying and freeing us, our avarice imprisons us. Why?

For one thing, our insatiable desire for more grows because unseen forces cleverly and subtly feed it. I once had a conversation with the owner and film editor of a multimillion-dollar television advertising firm that had a part in creating some of the famous commercials that run during Super Bowl football games. This annual television event commands millions of dollars per minute of airplay. It is not uncommon for a single sixty-second Super Bowl commercial to be the culmination of a hundred or more hours of actual video that never make it into the commercial. This means that the thirty to sixty seconds that do end up on the screen represent the most persuasive minds in the industry devising the most enticing images and music to lure you, the consumer, into buying the product. That is a powerful draw on the senses and the soul.

Advertising is one of the chief methods used to draw us deeper into our prisons of greed. Madison Avenue hawks goods and services in ways that make us yearn for what others have. Advertisers can make a light beer look like the fountain of "cool." They convince us that a clothing line can provide escape from our poor self-images. And a new automobile becomes the means by which we can cruise down that perfect road into a sunset of prestige and class. But the really shrewd part is that, come next season, there will be a new light beer, a sexier look, and a better car required to maintain the image. Millions are sucked into this vacuum of want, living in a perpetual state of longing.

SATISFACTION GUARANTEED

Your Greatest Treasure

Jesus said, "It is more blessed to give than to receive" (Acts 20:35). This paradox about possessions is especially ironic. It suggests that somehow we can get more from releasing and giving away than we can from receiving or holding tightly to what we have. Jesus is not talking about some mere psychic payoff, promising warm feelings every time we give. In fact, Jesus suggests elsewhere, like in the Beatitudes in Matthew 5, that the happiness that comes from God will sometimes come at a painful cost to us. So what did Jesus mean? And what kind of giving is Jesus talking about?

It's significant that Jesus is not merely talking about financial giving, an area that certainly exposes our priorities. Where we spend our money is a genuine barometer of our values. People need not talk about what they treasure and appreciate; they need only show their checkbook or credit card statement.

But our finances and material possessions are not our only resource. Time is another: a middle-aged unwed mother with four children may yearn to recapture her squandered youth. Experiences are a prized resource: millionaires have spent eyebrow-raising amounts of wealth to travel for just a few moments outside of the earth's atmosphere. Our health is precious: kings and presidents have said they would give away all their wealth and power for just one more year of life.

But Jesus is not interested in a particular kind of treasure. In fact, he is not interested in our treasure at all. His concern is *us*. We are his treasure. He focuses on our resources because he knows that he does not fully have our hearts unless we are willing to give up our resources to follow him. Once a rich young ruler (a prince perhaps) came to Jesus and said he wanted to be one

PARADOXY

of his disciples. Jesus responded by giving that man a shocking directive. "There is still one thing lacking," Jesus told the man. "Sell all that you own and distribute the money to the poor, and you will have treasure in heaven; then come, follow me." But when the man heard this, "he became sad, for he was very rich" (Luke 18:22–23 NRSV).

Jesus knew he could have a rich man's commitment and yet not have his love and friendship. He could have a listener's attention without having her interest. He could have their presence but not have their loyalty. That's why Jesus made the penetrating statement to his disciples, "For where your treasure is, there your heart will be also" (Matt. 6:21).

Our attitude toward giving is crucial because Jesus wants us to demonstrate with our lives that God matters more to us than even our greatest treasures. With that understood, how do we measure up as givers?

American Generosity?

By most estimates, America today is the wealthiest country in the history of the world. Let's examine what we do with all of our wealth, especially how much of our wealth we share with others. Or, to put it another way, let's see what this extraordinary wealth has produced in us.

What are we Americans like as givers? Some interesting information about the giving habits of Americans came to light in a study by the Rockefeller Brothers Fund.[1] This study revealed that Americans contribute an average of $650 a year to charities. Thirty-eight percent of the respondents thought they should be giving more than they now do to nonprofit institutions or causes.

Asked why they didn't, 23 percent said they "simply didn't get around to it" and 14 percent claimed they were never asked.

Eighty-one percent of all Americans believe it is the responsibility of people to give what they can to charities. Religious believers, according to the survey, were the undisputed winners in charitable contributions; 72 percent of all donated money was given by those who said they were motivated by religious faith.

Although believers give the most, how many give sacrificially? Certainly, some do. However, according to a 2003 survey by the Barna Group, even among conservative Christians who typically give the most, 18 percent of Christians who considered themselves "born again" gave no money to a church in 2003, and only 7 percent of them tithed to a church.[2] *World* magazine reported on charitable giving in a post–9/11 article, quoting Empty Tomb, a research group based in Champaign, Illinois:

> Protestant denominations have published data on an ongoing basis throughout the century. In 1916, Protestants were giving 2.9 percent of their incomes to their churches. In 1933, the depth of the Great Depression, it was 3.2 percent. In 1955, just after affluence began springing up through our culture, it was still 3.2 percent. By 1999, when Americans were overall much richer, after taxes and inflation, than in the Great Depression, Protestants were giving 2.6 percent of their incomes to their churches.[3]

The article added,

> The evidence is loud and clear that all apart from 9/11, and all apart from a puny stock market, Christians in America know very little about serious giving. The problem didn't hit us last September, and it didn't come via Enron or WorldCom. The problem lies deep in our own stingy hearts.[4]

PARADOXY

This is not intended to make anyone feel guilty who has not yet developed avid giving habits. Most of us don't live up to who we'd like to be in one area or another. One of my favorite prayers says, "Lord, please make me the kind of person that my *dog* thinks I am." Becoming a giver, financial or otherwise, is part of spiritual maturity. And spiritual maturity takes time; it's a process.

I raise these facts because they are an honest mirror of how we have responded to our wealth. Wealth has not made us a giving people. Personally, I'm not always proud of my own reflection in that mirror. But if I am to become generous like Jesus, if I am to find the blessedness that Jesus promised those who become givers, the process will not begin until I look humbly at the facts of how much I actually give. If I am to become like Jesus, I must start with the brutal recognition that I am *not* like him right now. No matter who we are—retiree, child, graduate student, professional, janitor, heiress, secretary, police officer, attorney, whatever—God wants us to become givers of life. And we start by facing the hard facts.

The Animal Just Below the Surface

The problem is that, rather than praying to become true givers, more often than not we maintain an unending desire for more. The truth is that we have an undeniable propensity toward greed. Why is this?

We learn greed or generosity in part from those who raise us. We teach habits to one another—especially to small children—without even knowing it. When it comes to the spiritual development of another's charity, we should never underestimate the power of our influence on those in our homes. Parents influence kids to give.

Brothers persuade sisters to share. Grandparents can influence us all to be free with our possessions. Even the charitable spirit of children often persuades adults to follow suit. But the reverse is also true: greed begets greed.

Twin brothers, Claude and Paul, lived in a small town called Les Cayes at the west end of Haiti where I worked for a number of months. They seemed as nervous as the rest of the town when a series of burglaries broke out. As in most of Haiti, the residents of Les Cayes had little to steal. But what they had was more precious than most of us in the wealthy Western world can imagine. An extra shirt, a cooking pot and some utensils, or a few tools to use for a trade meant the difference between having warmth, a meal, or a job and having nothing. Such things were essential for survival in a harshly competitive environment. So the rash of burglaries in Les Cayes was alarming.

The twin brothers, who were orphaned as boys, were now in their early twenties. They lived in a small branch and stucco hut on the edge of town. During the spate of burglaries, Claude appeared especially nervous. The whole town knew that he protected his belongings in a cabinet in their hut that he kept under padlock. Early one morning our small corner of town was driven into even edgier concern when we woke to the disturbing news that Claude's brother, Paul, was found unconscious in his bed, severely injured from multiple stab wounds. He was shuttled to a hospital several miles away. When he didn't return for many weeks, news came back that Paul was near death.

Fortunately, he did not die, and I will never forget the day that Paul returned. He was brought home in the back of a truck. He was still weak and recuperating; he needed the help of several friends even to get out of the vehicle. Claude came out as he heard the approach of the party that accompanied Paul. Claude flung open the door. However, rather than a shout for joy at his brother's recovery and return, Claude began to scream hysterically as if he'd seen a zombie. He was inconsolable. And his hysteria raised the suspicion of everyone in town, including the local police.

The police went to Claude and Paul's home and demanded to look inside the cabinet that Claude guarded so possessively. There they found all of the items that the townspeople had reported stolen in prior months. Claude was arrested and taken to a local jail where he was interrogated. In a confession to the police, Claude admitted that he had become agitated and angry when his brother insisted on seeing the contents of Claude's cabinet. To silence him, Claude attempted to murder him, his own brother, in the dark while he slept.

It was a vivid lesson: greed has the capacity to trump trust. And when confronted with surroundings that encourage a "survival of the fittest" mentality rather than an altruistic concern for others, we can easily develop a ruthless frame of mind.

We Feed Our Greed

Is human greed diminished as we accumulate more? Do those with greater wealth experience less greed? The affluent may appear to behave with less overt violence toward competitors. But at its heart, the passive-aggressive greed of the wealthiest may only mask a quieter avarice that clings to possessions just as tenaciously. All the while, the wealthy who are greedy ignore the masses who go without the basic needs of life.

The Old Testament author of the wisdom book Ecclesiastes knew about our insatiable desires all too well. He writes, "The lover of money will not be satisfied with money; nor the lover of wealth, with gain. This also is vanity" (5:10). What ancient biblical authors preached so long ago is true for the human race: when nourished, our hunger for money and possessions will overpower all other considerations.

Comparatively few in the world have the basic needs of life, let alone the luxuries that make life pleasant for many of us in the West. In their book *Fearfully and Wonderfully Made*, Dr. Paul Brand and Philip Yancey give our greed a context:

> Consider the world as if it were shrunk down to a community of 1000 persons: In our town of 1000—180 of us live high on a hill called the developed world; 820 live on the rocky bottom land called the rest of the world. The fortunate 180 on the hill have 80 percent of the wealth . . . 85 percent of all the automobiles, 80 percent of all the TV sets, 93 percent of all the telephones, and an average income of $5000 per person per year.
>
> The not-so-fortunate 820 people on the bottom get by on only $75–700 per person per year. They average five persons to a room.
>
> . . . The fortunate group of hill-dwellers . . . spend[s] less than 1 percent of their income to aid the lower land. In the United States, for example, of every $100 earned[, we spend 1/3 of that amount on] . . . recreation and amusement . . . clothes . . . alcohol and . . . tobacco. $1.30 is given for religious and charitable uses.[5]

We in the developed West often feel as though we are generous and frequent givers. Some are. But the sheer scale of our wealth so dwarfs the rest of the world that what the wealthy have versus what the poor do not have is incomprehensible to both. One of the thousands of orphaned children in the streets of a place like Addis Ababa, Ethiopia, cannot fathom how much we, the average U.S. citizen, eat every day, and we cannot grasp how little it would take to feed her.

Miser-able

It is not coincidence that the word *miserable* (from the Latin *miserabilis*, meaning "wretched, sad, or mournful") has its root in the word *miser*—what we know as an unpleasant person who grasps and hoards his or her possessions. Our materialism leaves us with more stuff, less personal satisfaction, and a never-ending, gnawing desire for more, more, more.

Some years ago PBS aired a special on the greed of America entitled *Affluenza*. It described how swollen expectations, hyper-commercialism, and shopping fever have resulted in an epidemic of bankruptcies, fractured families, and chronic stress in American society. The producers of the program explained, "This is a look at one of the greatest social maladies of our time: overconsumption and materialism. *Affluenza* explores one of the most sobering aspects of our consumerism and its enormous negative impact on our families, communities, and the environment."[6]

For most of us, in one area or another, our greed has no off button. Despite the lack of satisfaction that our possessions and gain consistently bring, we nevertheless seem to live as though the gadgets and toys, the vacations and timeshares, the furniture and clothing, all will eventually change our lives for the better when we attain enough of them.

A top-selling book of the 1990s, *How to Want What You Have* by Dr. Timothy Miller, teaches us that our psychological makeup is such that we will *always want more*. For the vast majority of us, no matter what we attain, we are not satisfied in the really

SATISFACTION GUARANTEED

deep ways that we want to be. Ironically, our avarice leads us to cycles of depression rather than to joy, and we measure our lives by what we have in our garages, bank accounts, and portfolios, rather than by who we are in character, charity, and integrity.

Jesus' Paradox: "Give to Receive"

Jesus Christ clearly understands our greedy nature, our endless desire for more. Yet in his statement quoted in Acts 20:35—"It is more blessed to give than to receive"—it is evident he does not intend to deprive us. We see this in a couple of significant ways. First, notice the emphasis: Jesus says it is *more* blessed to give than to receive; he does not say it is not a blessing to receive. It is obviously wonderful to get things that we like and enjoy. This makes his statement all the more powerful, because if we know the pleasure of getting good gifts, then we can imagine the great gift we receive from giving.

Second, Jesus wants us to have what we want, namely, happiness. The word Jesus uses for "blessed" was a familiar one in his day. Earlier Greek authors, such as Homer, used it as synonymous with "rich." If Jesus has that familiar meaning in mind, his paradox here has even more layers—"It is *richer* to give than receive." The word was also used to describe the Greek gods as being happy within themselves because they were not restrained by the natural and social laws of the human world. They were superfree. Jesus is describing the state of happiness that God wants for us—a happiness that is richer than wealth; a joy that is not bound and limited by human circumstances.

In Jesus' teachings about money and possessions, he rightly implies that what we want is not the money, the cars, the trips, the

PARADOXY

multiple houses, the boats, or the bank accounts. We do not even really want the friends, fame, or status that we think those things will bring. What we're truly looking for in our state of greed is the elusive quality of happiness that we often call *gratification*—the condition of being pleased and satisfied.

Actually, our greed is a selfishly twisted version of a gift—our God-implanted longing to know him. What we really long for is to be in ultimate communion with God. The psalmist wrote, "Delight yourself in the Lord and he will give you the desires of your heart" (Ps. 37:4). The implication is clear. The desires of our heart are synonymous with delighting ourselves in the Lord. Draw close to God and our longing hearts become satisfied.

If you think about it, this just makes sense. We work for the money we need to purchase cars, houses, educations; our lifelong chase for all these things is only a means to the greater end—the gratification that we long for in attaining them.

This is not to say that one cannot have both riches and happiness. But according to Jesus, happiness comes not as a result of material gain but from becoming like God, who is generous and giving. When we focus exclusively on mammon (the New Testament word for worldly possessions and gain), it only increases our desire for more. We chase after it and never catch it, like the mechanical rabbit on the rail that leads racing dogs around the track. And the faster we run, the faster the mechanical rabbit of mammon goes.

The emptiness in the pursuit of materialism for its own sake is evident whenever we get something or achieve some new economic level, yet we have no one to share it with. Even the greatest attainments of wealth or achievement are meaningless unless they are accompanied by loved ones who help imbue them with meaning in the contexts of our lives.

As the story goes, a minister woke up on a Sunday morning and realized that it was an exceptionally beautiful and sunny spring day. He decided he just had to play golf. So he telephoned the associate pastor, told him that he was feeling sick, and convinced his associate to do the church service for him that day. As soon as he hung up, the pastor headed out of town to a golf course several miles away to insure that he wouldn't accidentally run into anyone from his parish. All alone on that glorious early spring day, he set up on the first tee.

About this time, Peter leaned over to the Lord while looking down from heaven and exclaimed, "You're not going to let him get away with this, are you?" The Lord sighed, and said, "No, I guess not." Just then the minister hit the ball and it shot straight toward the pin. It dropped on the green just short of it, rolled up, and fell into the hole. It was a 410-yard hole in one! Peter was astonished. He looked at God and asked incredulously, "Why did you let him do *that*?" The Lord smiled and replied, "Who's he going to tell?"

Meyer once wrote, "God has set Eternity in our heart, and man's infinite capacity cannot be filled or satisfied with the things of time and sense."[7] True gratification and happiness come only in the context of meaningful and cherished relationships with others and with God. A lawyer once asked Jesus, "Teacher, which commandment in the law is the greatest?" Jesus responded, "'You shall love the Lord your God with all your heart, and with all your soul, and with all your mind.' This is the greatest and first commandment. And a second is like it: 'You shall love your neighbor as yourself.' On these two commandments hang all the law and the prophets" (Matt. 22:36–40 NRSV).

Moreover, Jesus often quoted and affirmed the Old Testament prophet Isaiah. Jesus was undoubtedly familiar with Isaiah's rhe-

PARADOXY

torical statement from God which spoke about attainments that *truly* satisfy, saying, "Why spend money on what is not bread, and your labor on what does not satisfy? Listen, listen to me, and eat what is good, and your soul will delight in the richest of fare. Give ear and come to me; hear me, that your soul may live" (Isa. 55:2–3). The attainment of things brings joy when we pursue the goals that humans were designed to strive for, namely, authentic and meaningful relationships with God and others.

The Results of Becoming a Giver

According to Jesus' teaching about giving, that deep sense of peace and joyful contentment (being "blessed") comes from giving away and letting go of material gain, not from gripping tighter. Does becoming less, rather than more, preoccupied with self make us happier? Are we more satisfied when sharing our time, talents, and treasure, rather than hoarding them?

Certainly we see life examples that seem to support this paradox of Jesus. People make immense sacrifices for causes they are passionate about, yet their lives are filled with meaning and they find great happiness in living their passions. Conversely, lottery winners become wealthy overnight, yet many become miserable. Scientific findings concur with what Jesus taught about giving and getting. Studies performed in psychology at major graduate universities have determined that "life-satisfaction occurs most often when people are engaged in absorbing activities that cause them to forget themselves, lose track of time and stop worrying."[8] Conversely, experts tell us that "materialism is toxic for happiness."[9] Even rich materialists aren't as happy as those who care less about getting and spending.

In the Gospel of Luke, Jesus explains further how we receive when we give, particularly when we give even at great personal cost. He says, "Give, and it will be given to you. A good measure, pressed down, shaken together and running over, will be poured into your lap. For with the measure you use, it will be measured to you" (6:38).

It is both noteworthy and tragic that this and other teachings of Jesus have been construed as "prosperity theology"—giving merely in order to get something in return from God. This is decidedly *not* what Jesus teaches. Jesus says in that same context, "If you lend to those from whom you hope to receive, what credit is that to you? Even sinners lend to sinners, to receive as much again. But love your enemies, do good, and lend, expecting nothing in return. Your reward will be great, and you will be children of the Most High" (Luke 6:34–35 NRSV).

Jesus' point is simply this: lending and expecting nothing in return is called *giving*! That means we're not in it for the payoff. Jesus' teachings on giving are not an instruction on how to do business. They are not about quid pro quo. Rather, Jesus' assertion that his followers should give, and it will be given to them, is more a statement about how people behave when they really know God and become the giving people that God wants them to be.

What, then, is Jesus talking about when he says that givers receive in "good measure, pressed down, shaken together"? Again, Jesus is simply stating a fact about the reality of how God provides for his own. He is reassuring people that when they follow God in becoming generous, they demonstrate that the God of the cosmos abides in and with them. Their acts of generosity don't gain them rewards; they simply reflect the spiritual reality already present in their lives. Those acts occur precisely *because* they are already sons and daughters of the Most High God. When we give, God not only provides for us as his children but abides with us as well. Perhaps no other biblical text says this more clearly than the first letter of John: "If anyone has material possessions and sees his brother in need but has no pity on him, how can the love of God be in him? Dear children, let us not love with words or tongue but with actions and in truth. This then is how we know that we belong to the truth, and how we set our hearts at rest in [God's] presence" (3:17–19).

Are givers "blessed," or made happy, as Jesus said they would be in Acts? I suspect that each person will have to determine this for himself or herself. But from my experience I can answer with an unequivocal yes. I have not known a generous person to complain about how much money it takes to feed the hungry at a homeless shelter or to provide basic necessities for those at a refugee station in a third-world country. Miserly people, on the other hand, often complain about how much it takes. Generous people often express concern that they don't or can't do more for others. Selfish people whine that they don't have enough time or money for themselves.

In my experience, generous families are generally happier families. But many stingy families whom I have known, even very wealthy ones with all the modern toys and conveniences that one could want, frequently seem troubled, unhappy, and internally conflicted.

There appears to be a direct connection between the vitality of our generosity and our level of happiness. Those whom I have known to give generously have been some of the most delightful to be around. Just the reverse is true of nongivers. Giving teaches us that our worth transcends our wallets and that the work of our lives is worth far more than its cash value.

Camels, Needle Eyes, and Idolatry

If Jesus' teaching is true—that giving brings real happiness—then why does it seem so elusive? Why doesn't this principle sink in with age or education? Christians may give lip service to it—that giving brings real joy—but many don't live it. In fact, they twist Scripture to justify how they live, missing Jesus' point entirely.

There are at least two interpretations of Jesus' saying in Matthew 19:24 (also in Luke 18:25): "It is easier for a camel to go through the eye of a needle than for someone who is rich to enter the kingdom of God." The first is based on claim that a gate exists somewhere in the city of Jerusalem that is so low that the only way a camel could get through it is to kneel down and crawl through. That interpretation fits so tidily into many other Christian understandings of sin, love of money, humility, and giving our burdens to God. But it is almost surely more of an urban legend than a historical fact.

I have found no credible evidence that such a gate ever existed in Jerusalem in Jesus' time. I suspect that interpretation says a lot more about our desire to explain away what we in the wealthy West are so uncomfortable with, namely, our gnawing hunger to have our cake and eat it too. If this eye of the needle was a small gate that a camel could squeeze through, then some rich people can enter the kingdom too. I can be rich and justify any lifestyle, as long as I tell myself, "But I'm still humble in my heart." I can feel comfortable while I sit in my European luxury sedan drinking my latte on my way to the red carpet event after visiting with my financial advisor whose advice I sought to assure me that I have nothing to worry about. My future is secure.

PARADOXY

I've diversified my portfolio and invested well. And besides, I'm a Christian. Nothing can touch me now.

We don't even want to think about the other possible interpretation of that saying of Jesus—that he really was hostile toward wealth. He couldn't possibly mean that wealth is one of life's fog screens, clouding our spiritual vision so that we can't see our need for God or everything that matters here and in eternity . . . could he?

Surely Jesus was implying that even the wealthy can get into heaven, so long as they are humble at the right times and do not flaunt their wealth, or better yet, they give generously to advance Christian causes. Right?

The only thing more misguided than the mental gymnastics required for that kind of internal wrangling over those words of Jesus is the reason behind it. We want to minimize our conflict over claiming to follow Jesus while living a life that is antithetical to everything he stood for. We want to maintain our sense of pride in everything we've worked for, including our moral goodness that God surely appreciates, and believe that it must count for something spiritually.

Such theorizing is baseless. And the irony is that urban legends exist to express and ease our collective fears about our world. Their purpose is to entertain and shock. But the only shocking thing about Jesus' statement is that he really meant just what he said—we *can't* have it all. Having and holding on to wealth indicates a love of wealth. And a love of wealth is a clear indicator of idolatry, which separates us from God. Is wealth the problem? Technically, no. Idolatry is. But Jesus specifically cited wealth as one of the significant barriers that keeps us from God because we delude ourselves about its power to seduce us. We want to say, "Well, you can have wealth; just don't love it." Jesus intimated,

SATISFACTION GUARANTEED

"No, you can't be a person who has wealth, holds on to it, lives for it, spends your life sweating to get it and keep it. You can't give it now and then, making sure that you always have more than the masses who don't know how to handle it as well as you. You can't do all of these things to claim the title that you so welcome—'rich'—and still say that you 'love the Lord your God with all your heart and with all your soul and with all your mind.'"

Is there any hope? That's what Jesus' disciples wondered in the face of that spiritual barrage. The verse following Jesus' saying tells us, "When the disciples heard this, they were greatly astonished and asked, 'Who then can be saved?'" Jesus' next words give us the hope we need (including those of us who try to sidestep his harsher sayings): "For mortals it is impossible, but for God all things are possible" (Matt. 19:25–26 NRSV).

Our moral and spiritual failures cause us to adjust our interpretations of Jesus' sayings to our comfort level. This affects every arena of life, including the ways that we allow money and possessions to possess us. All the denial in the world, Jesus suggests, won't fix that. We can't live in, or even strive to live in, the comfort of multimillion-dollar homes while most of the world lives in boxes and rags, and still claim that our professed indifference toward our wealth or what we deem to be reasonable generosity pleases God. Jesus wants us to do more than kneel down like camels in low doorways. He tells us that camels walking through needles' eyes and people who idolize anything above God (which is *all* of us), yet still claim to please him, are laughable.

The good news is that God's seemingly impossible love for selfish, self-deceived people like us is neither impossible nor laughable. It's real, and it's our only hope.

PARADOXY

Letting Go of What Is Not Yours

Perhaps more than any other of Jesus' paradoxes, his teaching on giving to receive is the most difficult. Like the others, it is not so much difficult to understand as it is difficult to really trust and submit to, in obedience to God. Money, possessions, time, talents, education, reputation—they are so tangible, important, and immediate in our daily lives that we find it easier to tighten our grip on them than to loosen it.

I am convinced that the real secret to finding Jesus' blessedness in giving is in seeing the world in a new way—in the way Jesus sees it. All that we have and all that we are belongs to God. Jesus, who repeatedly affirmed the authority of the Old Testament during his earthly ministry, knew of Scriptures like the prayer of Israel's King David recorded in 1 Chronicles 29:10–11: "Blessed are you, O LORD, the God of our ancestor Israel, forever and ever. Yours, O LORD, are the greatness, the power, the glory, the victory, and the majesty; for all that is in the heavens and on the earth is yours" (NRSV). Our relationship to things in the world becomes clear when we realize God's preexistent ownership of all things. Our burning temptation toward greed is extinguished when we obey God's call to become generous people and esteem God and people more highly than our desire for things. A preacher paints a picture of this in his sermon:

> You remember when they had old-fashioned Sunday School picnics? I do. As I recall it was back in the olden days. . . . They said, we'll all meet at Sycamore Lodge at Shelby Park at 4:30 on Saturday. You bring your supper and we'll furnish the ice tea. But if you were like me, when you came home at the last

minute and got ready to pack your picnic all you could find in the fridge was one dried up piece of bologna and just enough mustard in the bottom of the jar so that you got it all over your knuckles trying to get to it. And just two slices of stale bread to go with it.

So you made your bologna sandwich, wrapped it in an old brown bag, and went to the picnic. And when it came time to eat you sat at the end of a table and spread out a sandwich but the folks who sat next to you brought a feast. The lady was a good cook and she had worked hard all day to get ready for the picnic. She had fried chicken and baked beans, potato salad and homemade rolls, sliced tomatoes, pickles, olives, and celery. Two big homemade chocolate pies to top it off. That's what they spread out next to you as you sat there with your bologna sandwich.

And then they said to you, "Why don't we just put it all together?"

"I couldn't even think of it," you murmured in embarrassment with one eye on the chicken.

"Ah, come on. There's plenty of chicken, plenty of pie, plenty of everything. And we *love* bologna. Let's just put it all together."

And so you did and there you sat eating like a king when you came like a pauper.

One day it dawned on me that God had been saying just that sort of thing to me.

"Why don't you take what you have and what you are, and I'll take what I have and what I am and we'll put it all together."

I began to see that when I put what I was and am and hope to be with what God is, I had stumbled upon the bargain of a lifetime. I get to thinking sometimes of *me* sharing with *God*. When I think of how little I bring and how much God brings and then invites me to share, I know that I should be shouting

PARADOXY

to the housetops. But I'm so filled with awe and wonder that I can hardly speak.

God has all things in abundance and God says, "Let's just put it all together." And when I think about that it really amuses me to see someone running along through life, hanging onto their dumb bag with that stale bologna sandwich in it, saying, *"GOD'S NOT GONNA GET MY SANDWICH!"*[10]

When we finally admit how little we come to the table with, and how much God offers to provide, only then can we be gratified. Only then do we stand in the place that we must in order to receive God's blessing when we give.

Meditation

I do not thank thee, Lord,
that I have bread to eat while others starve;
nor yet for work to do
while empty hands solicit heaven;
nor for a body strong
while other bodies flatten beds of pain.
No, not for these do I give thanks.

But I am grateful, Lord,
because my meager loaf I may divide;
for that my busy hands
may move to meet another's need;
because my doubled strength
I may expend to steady one who faints.
Yes, for all these do I give thanks!

For heart to share,
desire to bear,
and will to live,
flamed into one
by deathless Love—
Thanks be to God for this.
Unspeakable! God's Gift.[11]

Jamie Alford

PARADOXY

5: Maximum Security Freedom

Be Enslaved to Be Free

If you hold to my teaching . . . then you will know the truth, and the truth will set you free.

Jesus

You gotta serve somebody.

Bob Dylan

One of Jesus' most powerful spiritual analogies for evil's effect on humanity is the analogy of human slavery. In John 8:34, Jesus said, "I tell you the truth, everyone who sins is a slave to sin." And given that Jesus fully endorsed the teachings of the Old Testament, he also knew that sin permeates the entire human race. No one is exempt (see, e.g., Pss. 14:1, 3; 53:1, 3).

But what did Jesus mean, we are *slaves* to sin? How does that play out in our lives? And even before we ask whether we can be freed from our slavery to sin, what does it mean that we are *all* under this spiritual servitude? We find keys to understanding Jesus' teachings on slavery and freedom when we are jarred with a contemporary glimpse of what experiencing slavery means for real people.

House Children

I stared back into the blank eyes of a little girl who sat with her brother against the back wall of a crude adobe house in a rural jungle area of Haiti. She and her brother did not smile. Their eyes were empty. Both of them seemed reasonably well fed, but their clothes were worn and old. The two only moved about when told to, and then they operated like robots, obeying the brusque orders of the mother and father who owned the house.

These children's status was the result of a cultural practice that existed in the mid-1980s in several regions in Haiti because of the poverty and high mortality rate of adults. Haiti has been identified as the poorest country in the Western Hemisphere. When parents died, their children were sent or sometimes voluntarily went to a relative or neighbor who agreed to take them in. However, most adults could not afford to take on more mouths to feed, minds to educate, or bodies to clothe. The result was that these children entered homes where they received only the bare essentials to survive. They were expected to work for the family, who kept them at emotional and physical arm's length.

The Haitian Creole term for such children was *house children.* Their status was little more than indentured household slaves. Haitian adults housing such children explained to me the unwritten rule that these children were not to be touched or spoken

PARADOXY

to affectionately. They typically lived behind the house, either in a shed or sometimes under a simple lean-to. They took their meals by themselves and otherwise lived a life of doing chores on demand. I had heard about many instances of abuse of these house children.

As I sat at a table talking to the father of the family where the little girl with the blank eyes lived, I said "hi" to her and asked in Creole what her name was. She stared at the floor, a wary expression of fearfulness on her face. To my distress, the father sternly demanded that she respond. She shuffled over to me and extended a limp hand for me to shake, never looking up from the floor.

When I questioned the family about it later, they argued the rationale for such treatment of house children. Families with such kids cannot afford to raise them as their own and certainly cannot afford to send them to elementary school, which at that time would have cost about twelve dollars per month and would have provided them with a new, clean school uniform and a daily meal. The parents of house children cannot promise them much of a future, so why get their hopes up? They should be grateful, so the argument went, to have a place to stay and meals to sustain them.

I countered their arguments, decrying as persuasively as I could their innocent and young status, as well as the lack of compassion in the house child practice. But it was an uphill battle, always met with the same rejoinder: as a wealthy American, I could not possibly understand.

Why Slaves Stay Slaves

Why did the Haitian house children not leave their situations? Some house children in Haiti remained in some homes under

MAXIMUM SECURITY FREEDOM

threat of violence if they tried to leave. But not all children were held under such threats. So why did they stay to live, not like children, but like slaves? What was the mental or emotional slavery that kept them there?

A couple of things seemed especially apparent. First, the house children whom I saw were usually very young when they were orphaned. Those who housed, indeed held, them took advantage of the child's inability to reason or rise above their circumstances to understand just how bad things were. Second, where would they go? Haiti is a profoundly poor place. In the capital city of Port au Prince, square miles of tin, wood, and cardboard shacks and boxes stand atop one another as homes for tens of thousands of poverty-stricken people. Raw sewage runs in the narrow streets of those barrios. And children are at the low end of the social totem pole. In a societal context so unyielding, a house child would understandably look at his or her situation and simply conclude, it's just the way things are.

As I flew back to the United States after living in Haiti for several months, I stared out the window. Seven hundred miles. Just seven hundred miles off the coast of one of the world's wealthiest countries. That's how far Haiti is from Miami. If the Haitians living in their poverty only knew. Yet after living and working among the Haitian people, watching their hardships, rubbing shoulders with them in their burdensome poverty, and seeing their desperation now juxtaposed to the lavish wealth of even the average American on that airplane, I was threatened by fatalistic hopelessness for the Haitians' circumstances. I could do little more than weep for them. And that I did.

PARADOXY

Though I have come to believe that we should have hope to battle the oppression of even the most desperate poverty, one real consequence of slavery is the bending of human reality into the hopeless conviction that life cannot change. The intensity of such oppression deflates and demoralizes the human spirit so that nearly all affected by it conclude that no one will come to ease the suffering, no one has the power to break those strong bonds of oppression, and no one will care enough to pull those so afflicted from that pit.

The good news, of course, is that such fatalistic conclusions do not have to be true. Redemption is possible. Slaves can be set free.

Spiritual Slaves, Physical Slaves

In the same way that physical human slavery crushes the human spirit unless the captives are set free, Jesus recognized our need to be set free from our spiritual slavery. His analogy about our slavery to sin bears a striking resemblance to the circumstances of the house children of Haiti. In John 8:34–36, Jesus told some religious leaders, "I tell you the truth, everyone who sins is a slave to sin. Now a slave has no permanent place in the family, but a son belongs to it forever. So if the Son sets you free, you will be free indeed."

Jesus wasn't endorsing the institution of slavery. He was stating a fact about what it was like to be a slave. Slaves may live in a house, but that doesn't make it their home. They may interact with the residents, but they are not members of the family. Similarly, being slaves to sin robs us from being insiders in the family of God.

But is the human condition really as spiritually dire as Jesus suggests? Are we really slaves to sin? Or has he overstated his case?

Freedom Leads to Slavery

Spiritually and morally, we may think that we do as we like, often living selfishly against the character of God. But when we live that way, we aren't free at all. Instead, we become slaves to our own way of life.

When Jesus suggested that all of us are "slaves to sin," his use of the word "slaves" had palpable connotations to his listeners. No doubt they had seen the so-called life of slaves. Many were brought into the centers of the Greco-Roman towns of Jesus' day riding in carts and locked in chains. They were taken to the agora, the main town square, where vendors sold fresh fish, goat meat, fruit, or vegetables under stands covered with goatskin or canvas tarps. Auctions of various kinds were often held in the center of the agora, and slave sales were common in such public markets.

The ruins of ancient agoras have revealed that it was common for slave traders to stand slaves up on a pedestal and invite potential buyers to come, look, and bid on them. Slaves were property, valued no more than livestock or commodities. The slaves and the costs to keep them are recorded in untold numbers of dusty papyri fragments—the costs of their clothes, breakfasts, incidentals were often listed along with the other business expenses in budgets that also recorded the costs to feed and care for horses, to purchase grain, or to buy oils. Wills commonly listed slaves among what was left after a person died and bequeathed the slaves along with the rest of the property. Debtors paid their debts with slaves "same as cash" when it was agreeable to a creditor.

The picture of a slave in first-century Palestine was not one of dignity. It was not an image of a person but of mere chattel. The slave was a good and a service in one. Although a few owners occasionally regarded slaves with some dignity, that was rare. Jesus' life reflects great compassion for those of lowly status in his society, like slaves; at the same time, his description of those who are "slaves to sin" reflects his pity for us who have that spiritual status.

And isn't Jesus right? We so often live out patterns that lead us to pitiable lives. We resist what we know is right and indulge in what we openly affirm is wrong. Even when we *want* to live honorably, we seem to act in ways contrary to our desires. Our thoughts lead to actions, actions lead to habits, habits lead to addictions, and the consequences are often destructive to us and those around us.

Addiction to alcoholism, drugs, anger, sex, spending, or gambling are obvious cases in point. But even tamer habits often begin to control us and adversely affect our lives and relationships. We watch trivial television that we readily admit is a stellar waste of time. We squander endless hours on the Internet. We overeat, indulge in literary tripe, read or view pornography, or simply do *nothing* with precious time. These behaviors, allegedly resulting in "victimless crimes," become thin disguises for wasted lives.

Often we defend ourselves, claiming, "It's my business. I'm not bothering anyone else. It's simply how I relax." But it isn't true. It is the business of others. The hours that we waste away on Internet sites cost our children hours of bonding that never occur, time that can never be retrieved. Our choices affect those close to us. Our spouses, friends, and loved ones suffer, often quietly, in frustration at how we seem to know more about the fictitious lives of shallow sitcom characters than we do about them.

And in such lifestyles, we do not relax either internally in our spirits or externally in our aggravated and anemic relationships. On the contrary, we live in spiritual bondage. We are entrapped in personal prisons that we create for ourselves. We long for freedom from our self-made worlds, but we return to our masters regularly, like slaves, almost as if we don't know where else to turn. Our habitual behavior creates for us systems of rewards that do not reward at all. Instead, like a narcotic, each visit to our old ways of life demands more than before and gives less satisfaction than we had hoped.

St. Paul confesses to his own spiritual enslavement and inward spiritual warfare, and how those led him to an internal sense of personal imprisonment:

> I am unspiritual, sold as a slave to sin. I do not understand what I do. For what I want to do I do not do, but what I hate I do. . . . For I have the desire to do what is good, but I cannot carry it out. For what I do is not the good I want to do; no, the evil I do not want to do—this I keep on doing. . . .
>
> So I find this law at work: When I want to do good, evil is right there with me. For in my inner being I delight in God's law; but I see another law at work in the members of my body, waging war against the law of my mind and making me a prisoner of the law of sin at work within my members.
>
> Romans 7:14–15, 18b–19, 21–23

What we think is the freedom to live as we want leads to self-made spiritual confinement. And just when we think that things cannot get worse, the Bible tells us that they do.

The Law of Sin and Death

The problem with the enslavement to sin that Jesus describes is that it does not merely end there. Enslavement to sin eventually leads to what St. Paul describes as the "law of sin and death" (Rom. 8:2). Simply put, this means that as we drive ourselves ever deeper

PARADOXY

into our internal imprisonment, we do so to our own spiritual peril. In Romans 6:23 St. Paul says, "The payment for sin is death" (GOD'S WORD). The word "payment" here means "what is given in exchange for something." Death is the payment that we earn by living selfishly in sin. We merit death by working at sin.

We all experience spiritual bankruptcy and imprisonment at one point or another, whether or not we admit it. It is a painful reality. To experience spiritual freedom we must begin by admitting our problem rather than denying it. Honestly acknowledging our spiritual confinement is to take the first step in discovering the keys that can set us free.

Near the end of Romans 7 Paul describes his internal spiritual battle: "What a miserable man I am! Who will save me from this body that brings me death?" (v. 24 ICB). His honesty about his own sense of spiritual and moral captivity is palpable.

Jesus' words about our spiritual enslavement to sin paint a bleak picture. But he began that conversation about spiritual slavery only because he wanted to end it by offering the hope of spiritual freedom. Hence, Jesus said, "And you will know the truth, and the truth will make you free" (John 8:32 NRSV). The spiritual freedom that Jesus taught releases our stagnant spiritual restrictions in at least two ways—it gives us *freedom from* our past actions and habits that led to our slavery in the first place, and it gives us *freedom to* live life in new ways, as new creations with fresh outlooks.

Freedom from Slavery to Sin

Our slavery to sin is more than feelings of being trapped in bad habits. It entangles us with a deep sense of guilt and regret about how we have lived. It binds us in despair about how our actions have failed to build up our relationships with those we love and care for the most. The farther we travel through life, the more most of us regret aspects of our pasts. We would like the freedom to mend broken relationships, to take back harsh words, or to have time with loved ones that we now see we squandered away on endeavors that didn't much matter and were clearly of lesser importance. Ultimately, in our spiritual slavery, we incur moral and spiritual debts owed to one another and to God. For those debts to be paid, there must be forgiveness. Our past cannot be altered. In many cases we cannot obtain the forgiveness from others that we want and need. But we can find forgiveness from God. Ultimately, our sin is against him. And God's forgiveness is the decisive pardon that can relieve all guilt and ease the pain of our regrets.

The Freedom of Forgiveness

Forgiveness for our past is at the center of Jesus' mission and ministry. He was not a teacher who merely educated people on how to be good. Jesus was not interested in giving us tips on a better life, writing a great book, becoming a great historical figure, or even starting a religion. His mission was to become a slave himself and to offer his life as a sacrifice for the sins of all and thereby provide an avenue for God's forgiveness to all.

Early in Jesus' three-year ministry, he went with his disciples to Nazareth, the town where he was raised. He entered the synagogue there, walked to the main speaking platform, and read from an Old Testament scroll opened to the book of Isaiah. But Jesus did not just read from Isaiah. He made a scandalous interpretation of that book by implying that the prophet Isaiah was

PARADOXY

prophesying about *him*, Jesus, when Isaiah wrote, "The Spirit of the Lord is upon me, because he has anointed me to bring good news to the poor. He has sent me to proclaim release to the captives and recovery of sight to the blind, to let the oppressed go free" (Luke 4:18 NRSV). Jesus' allusions to freeing those held captive became an ongoing theme throughout his ministry, and its meaning became clearer in later teachings. In Matthew 20:27–28 (NRSV) Jesus conversed with his disciples, referring to himself as the Son of Man: "Whoever wishes to be first among you must be your slave; just as the Son of Man came not to be served but to serve, and to give his life a ransom for many." Jesus suggests that *he* would become the servant, the slave, whose act would bring freedom for those taken against their will.

Just as a kidnapper abducts a child and holds that child until a ransom is paid, humanity has been abducted and enslaved by sin. As we enslave ourselves with our own immoral and unspiritual acts against God and one another, we find ourselves conflicted. We may not want to live that way. Our actions create a debt. A ransom is demanded, and only a person with the currency of spiritual and moral purity can pay it and thereby set humanity free. Jesus—the "Son of Man"—had that currency.

Repeatedly throughout his ministry, Jesus laid claim both to deity and to the ability to forgive sin (see, e.g., Matt. 9:2, 6; Mark 2:5–11; Luke 5:20–25; 7:48–50). And because of his love for us and his single-mindedness to achieve forgiveness for humanity before God, Jesus gave his life as a sacrifice on the cross to pay the required ransom that can satisfy the debt. Even on the cross as he hung dying, he prayed for God's forgiveness for those who were crucifying him when he said, "Father, forgive them; for they do not know what they are doing" (Luke 23:34 NRSV). Spiritual freedom found in God's forgiveness is a gift given through the sacrifice of Jesus Christ. But gifts aren't much good when they're not accepted or opened to appreciate.

Every Christmas I receive some gifts that I like and one or two that I don't. The gifts that give me lasting impressions come from the heart of someone who either sacrificed in giving it to me or gave something to remind me of their powerfully significant place in my life.

I can hardly name five of the many presents that I received over the first twenty-one years of my life. But one stands out. When I graduated from college, my mom gave me a picture album of accumulated photographs of my family and me from the time I was little. She had taken months collecting and copying them from old photos lying around the house in boxes and stored away in closets. I have appreciated that gift over the years because of what it signifies. It represents a lifetime of my parents' care, nurture, and sacrifice for me as they raised me and my brother. It reminds me of my dear brother, Tim, with whom I wrestled and laughed and played as we grew up and became the best of friends. That photo album portrays those whom I have trusted with my life.

The cross is the most recognizable symbol in the world. Thousands wear one as jewelry, and for some, it is only an emblem. For others, the cross they wear is like my mom's gift of that photo album, a representation of their loved ones.

But for many, the cross represents Jesus' forgiveness and freedom. It is a powerful reminder of what he did to offer it to us and how much it cost. It's always moving for me to hear a person make that first connection in a prayer to become a Christian. They ask God for forgiveness and accept the sacrifice Jesus Christ made on their behalf. Time and again, I hear the unmistakable click of God's key unlocking the shackles of the sin and the

PARADOXY

thud of the chains falling to the ground. This release allows you and me to anticipate the next attribute that the freedom of Jesus promises—newness of life.

Freedom to Experience New Life

No matter how well life is going, when we are genuinely reflective we realize that we are all bound to pasts marked with mistakes, poor choices, times of selfish or foolish living, or bad experiences. We have areas of life that we would like a chance to do over. Certainly, we can look back and say, "I learned some good things even from those bad times." But then we spend our remaining days trying not to repeat those patterns. Our pasts can lock us into a quiet despair, dashing hopes for a new life. But according to Jesus, there is hope. Freedom from the past is possible.

In John 8:31–32, Jesus said, "If you hold to my teaching, . . . [t]hen you will know the truth, and the truth will set you free." The sacrifice of Jesus Christ can set us free from the *penalty* of our sin against God and others. But now Jesus tells us that our commitment to him can also set us free from the *practice* of sin that led us to that penalty in the first place. Jesus is not only the forgiver of failures for those who trust him, he is a model for those who will follow him.

This does not mean that we will ever stop sinning completely. Sin is the sad but ultimate mark left on the human race so long as we are bound by our mortal bodies. We need not live in hopeless resignation. We can experience positive change. We can have a brighter future. Jesus' paradox in John 8:31–32 tells us that we can experience the freedom to bind ourselves to a new way of life.

St. Paul describes it this way, "If anyone belongs to Christ, then he is made new. The old things have gone; everything is made new!" (2 Cor. 5:17 ICB). We can find that place of spiritual freedom that we long for, but we will only find it when we lock our lives into the ways of the Master—the ways of Jesus.

The word that Jesus uses in John 8:31 when he says, "Hold to my teaching" comes from a word commonly translated "to remain or endure at something." It's the same word that Jesus used in John 15:10 where he says, "If you obey my commands, you will remain in my love, just as I have obeyed my Father's commands and remain in his love."

The idea here is that Jesus himself was not above his own paradoxical teaching. He shows us by his example that we find our greatest spiritual freedom from the chains of our past and from the habits that have held us captive, not when we do what we want or when we live with some wild abandonment. We find true spiritual freedom when we submit our lives to the desires and unfathomable love of God and commit to imitate the self-sacrificial love that Jesus showed others.

Freedom to Continue to Sin?

As St. Paul began to spread the message of God's love for people as seen in the sacrifice of Jesus Christ on the cross, his listeners began to ask a question that has persisted through the ages: "If God loves us whether we sin or not, then why not continue to sin just as much as we please?"

The Old Testament is the record of the ancient Jews and their relationship to God. While it is the bedrock for understanding the New Testament, it also stands as an archetype for how so

PARADOXY

much of humanity has acted in relation to God, including later Christians.

The ancient Jews found themselves living and reliving a cycle that moved from physical bondage to spiritual faith from spiritual faith to courage and conviction, from courage and conviction to trust in God. This trust led them to act on God's directives that, in turn, brought about their freedom. But then this freedom led to abundance, abundance to selfishness, selfishness to complacency, complacency to apathy, apathy to indifference toward God and idolatrous dependence on surrounding nations. Finally, that dependence led back again into bondage.

We as individuals carry out our personal lives with similar patterns and cycles. We long for personal freedom and often begin to find it when we start down the road to spiritual commitment and trust in God. But so often we become quickly intoxicated with the sensations that our newfound freedom brings. We want to keep the *feelings* of freedom without keeping the commitments that led us to freedom in the first place. We only want to dabble in spiritual life. We have trouble keeping our focus. And soon we find that we want to use our newfound freedom to live, not according to God's self-sacrificial love, but according to our self-centered whims. The result is a series of expeditions down paths that eventually lead us back into the place of bondage from which we came—substance abuse, stealing from our workplaces, maligning others through gossip, ignoring our families, or just wasting our lives away.

Jesus' very life, however, was a paradox of freedom that he found in the maximum-security confinement of his commitment to God the Father's purposes and plans. It was centered on a love for God and for others that superseded all else. Jesus tells us that we too will only find our freedom in following his same path of commitment.

St. Paul put a fine point on this teaching in his first-century letter to the Christians in Galatia. He said, "For you were called to freedom, brothers and sisters; only do not use your freedom as an opportunity for self-indulgence, but through love become slaves to one another" (5:13 NRSV).

Back to the original question that we often want to ask: if God loves me no matter what, why shouldn't I accept that love and then be free to still live as I please? There are a couple of serious problems with this mindset.

First, doing as we please is *not* synonymous with true freedom. We sometimes talk about a bicycle wheel being free to spin on its axle. But we wouldn't say the same thing about that wheel being free to fall aimlessly on the ground. The wheel is free when it spins in the way that it was designed to spin. It can carry a rider only when it is held tightly to the axle by the nuts and bolts intended to keep it where it is supposed to be. Jesus' promise of freedom is not a promise of self-rule. It is a promise that we can live in the freedom that God's purposes and plans bring to us.

Second, demanding that we live as we want after experiencing the forgiving love of God through Jesus Christ is reentering spiritual slavery after God has set us free from it. We live so long and so thoroughly in our imprisonment to sin, including deeply rooted and insidiously destructive habits and addictions, and then we ask God for the very thing that will defeat the freedom he wants to give us. We say, "Can't I have God's freedom and love for me, and still live any way I want? Can't I have my cake and eat it too?"

Actually, it depends on what we mean by such questions. If we mean that we want to wallow in selfishness and still experience God's freedom, then no. We're missing what real freedom is, and we're injuring ourselves in the process. God's freedom is a freedom to pursue all that God wants us to be. It offers us

PARADOXY

something so much more valuable than what we chase after when we're enslaved to sin. When our lives are only self-seeking, we separate ourselves from meaning and significance.

If, on the other hand, we want to be free and truly enjoy life based on a changed understanding of what we want, then yes, we can have both of those.

Essentially, Jesus presumes humans are in one of two positions. Either we are slaves to sin and not free, or we are submitting to God and are free from sin and free to love and serve God. But in the second condition there are constraints. We cannot say, "I'm the boss of myself." God's freedom is the paradox of the joy of being enslaved to our reason for living.

British author D. H. Lawrence wrote,

> The freest are perhaps least free. Men are free when they are in a living homeland, not when they are straying and breaking away. Men are free when they are obeying some deep, inward voice of religious belief. Obeying from within. Men are free when they belong to a living, organic, believing community, active in fulfilling some unfulfilled, perhaps unrealized purpose. Not when they are escaping to some wild west. . . . Men are not free when they are doing just what they like. The moment you can do just what you like, there is nothing you care about doing.[1]

Paul raises and then addresses this issue in Romans 6:1–2 when he says, "So do you think that we should continue sinning so that God will give us more and more grace? No! We died to our old sinful lives. So how can we continue living with sin?" (ICB). Continuing to live selfishly, outside the love of God after experiencing and knowing the power and freedom of God's love, is like deliberately contracting a disease in order to demonstrate the power of antibiotics. But true spiritual freedom does not involve doing whatever I want to do. D. H. Lawrence is right; that is a bewildering kind of imprisonment. No, God's freedom, as we find it in the love and teachings of Jesus, means that I can be set free to attain all that God intended me to attain and to enjoy life to the outer reaches of my most hopeful dreams—but only when I remain fixed securely in the custody of God's ways and Christ's love.

Maximum Security Freedom

Is God's plan to forgive us really just a plan to entrap us into obligation to him? Is the apparent gift of Jesus' death on the cross really just a plan to bait us into a life of servitude rather than freedom? No. Why? Because God's call for us to serve by living out the love of Jesus toward a broken world—giving us meaningful, fulfilled lives—is just as much a gift to us as God's forgiveness for our sins was in the first place.

St. Augustine of Hippo (354–430) wrote, "He that is good is free, though he is a slave; he that is evil is a slave, though he be a king."[2] The problem with the question of whether God's love is really designed to entrap us into some kind of divine servitude is that it wrongly presumes that *not* serving God is freedom. That presumption is unequivocally false.

We can ignore God, but we will still have at least one master. If we decide to "liberate" our lives from God, we will be enslaved to our own changing whims, the endless demands of a job, or relationships wherein people ultimately let us down time and time again.

The masters we serve come in many forms—money, status, power, sex, mindless living, laziness, depression, hatred. However,

PARADOXY

as the teachings of Jesus reveal, serving any of those masters, while ignoring God, places us in personal prisons of lonely self-rule and eventual spiritual self-destruction. Without God, we live in increasing isolation without hope.

The greatest favor we can do for ourselves is not to seek freedom but to seek the right Master. Freedom does not come from simply exercising our will. Freedom comes when we make choices to follow our calling and true passions.

And so Jesus' paradox of freedom becomes clear. As a follower of God in Jesus Christ I *am* imprisoned to God. But that imprisonment is the very thing that gives me the greatest sense of hope-filled freedom. Paul often gladly introduced himself in his letters as "Paul, a prisoner of Christ Jesus" (Philem. 1). Likewise, the author of the book of James refers to himself as a "servant [or slave] of God and of the Lord Jesus Christ," as he opens his New Testament letter (1:1). Many scholars attribute the book of James to the half-brother of Jesus. To be sure, all who commit themselves to Jesus Christ become his prisoner as well.

What are the terms of the sentence for those who find themselves bound in servitude to God through Jesus Christ? We are sentenced to an infinite life filled with unconditional love. We will serve our time concurrently with the promise of God's peace in every circumstance. We are never eligible for parole to re-condemn ourselves for our past failures and faults, because they have been forgiven and forgotten by God, the ultimate Judge. Finally, we must abandon all hope of escaping from God, because "neither height nor depth, nor anything else in all creation, will be able to separate us from the love of God" and we "will dwell in the house of the LORD forever" (Rom. 8:39; Ps. 23:6).

Accepting God's forgiveness and becoming a disciple of Jesus Christ is a commitment to a kind of indentured servitude. It is accepting a life sentence of being shackled to God's grace. But living a lifetime in the shade of God's purpose, and experiencing God's love so strongly that I must share it with others, is like being sentenced to the Ritz Carlton in a tropical paradise. It is the spiritual version of jet service to any destination, unlimited food and drink, and maid service at any time. If this is God's divine slavery, if this is God's incarceration, then lock me up and throw away the key.

Meditation

Thanks that Your freedom is more than a matter of aimless choice; that it is not enough for me to affirm my liberty by choosing "something." Instead, Lord of life, may I use my freedom to choose something *Good*. Every morning, Lord, give me the courage to rise, and to choose You.

Adapted from Thomas Merton, *No Man Is an Island*[3]

PARADOXY

6: Against Your Better Judgment

Find Fool's Wisdom

For the message about the cross is foolishness to those who are perishing, but to us who are being saved it is the power of God. . . . For God's foolishness is wiser than human wisdom, and God's weakness is stronger than human strength.

St. Paul

It is unwise to be too sure of one's own wisdom. It is healthy to be reminded that the strongest might weaken and the wisest might err.

Mahatma Gandhi

I love to learn. Consequently, I have spent many years in graduate education at different institutions. Over the years I have run into a few professors who not only do not believe in God or spiritual realities, they seem to have a need to deride students in their classes who do. What has often struck me is how their barbed comments reflect a lack of understanding of what religious believers actually think, believe, say, or do.

One graduate course I took was Symbolic Logic, difficult but interesting. The professor who taught it was a Princeton graduate and very bright. He was also cynical and seemed to have a disdain for religion that surfaced without warning during his classes.

At the beginning of one class, one of the students had a book on a religious subject. I don't recall its content. The professor looked at it and, with a sarcastic smile, said, "Ah, read this, my son, and you'll be wiser." It was one of many flippant, biting comments that he made over the course of the semester. I wanted to ignore it. But the momentary uneasiness in the room revealed that his sarcasm genuinely annoyed the five or six of us who practiced lives of faith.

At first, I didn't know how to read my own internal reaction. I didn't want to make too much of it. But I did feel something. Was I offended? Not really. Instead, his statement just made me feel lousy; it's that simple. I felt bad because I thought highly of him in many ways, but he was mocking something that was really meaningful to me. I was also disappointed in his glib conclusion that any wisdom religion has to offer is a whimsical illusion. The really sad part was that it happened in the context of a university classroom—where knowledge and freedom of thought and exploration are supposed to prevail. This professor did not offer knowledge that debunked religion; he offered sarcastic misrepresentations that disgraced himself.

Is Wisdom Real?

If *knowledge* is the accumulation of information and experience, *wisdom* is the understanding of how best to use them. Many would accept this as true. They acknowledge that wisdom exists, and they wish for it. But they see it as unattainable, available only to the aged or spiritually enlightened.

Others, however, consider wisdom merely a convention. Wisdom, they argue, is ultimately only people's opinions. One of the twentieth century's renowned philosophers, Ludwig Wittgenstein, said, "It seems to me that in every culture, I come across a chapter headed 'Wisdom.' And then I know exactly what is going to follow: 'Vanity of vanities, all is vanity.'"[1] I sympathize with Wittgenstein. But if he is right about that in every instance, then he would have to apply it to his own claim as well. We may mock notions of wisdom as illusory. But we need only to experience a fool (who may turn out to be us) to realize that if fools truly exist, so must wisdom.

Do followers of Jesus Christ claim to be wiser than others? I don't think honest Christians do. No more so than a starving man who has been given bread claims to be the source of the bread. He can only point the way to where he got it. But many followers of Jesus do claim to have experienced glimpses of God's wisdom in Christ despite their own lives that are fraught with foolishness. God's wisdom is for Christians as ironic as God's love for us. We consistently fall short of God's ideals, and he still loves us. In the same manner, we live in ways that we regret, and we say with each passing stage of life, "If only I knew then what I know now." Yet God still invades our circumstances with unique insights that we come to know as his wisdom.

For me as a Christian, I have come to believe that wisdom is as real as the chair I am sitting in. It is not an illusion or a figment of an overactive spiritual imagination. The Old Testament writer of Proverbs personified it as a spiritual reality:

Wisdom calls aloud in the street,
    she raises her voice in the public squares;
at the head of the noisy streets she cries out,
    in the gateways of the city she makes her speech:
"How long will you simple ones love your simple ways?
    How long will mockers delight in mockery and
        fools hate knowledge? . . .
Since they hated knowledge and
        did not choose to fear the LORD,
    since they would not accept my advice
    and spurned my rebuke, they will eat the fruit of their ways
    and be filled with the fruit of their schemes.
For the waywardness of the simple will kill them,
    and the complacency of fools will destroy them;
but whoever listens to me will live in safety
    and be at ease, without fear of harm."

Proverbs 1:20–22, 29–33

Wisdom is as real as the immaturity and simple-mindedness is of those whom wisdom seeks to correct and protect. Wisdom is the standard against which we judge foolishness and fools.

Jesus in Training

Judging from Scripture, Jesus did not teach a paradox about wisdom with his words as much as he did with his life. And his

PARADOXY

earliest followers wrote about how he embodied true wisdom in his mission and even in his death by crucifixion. Since that time, both ancients and moderns, those who do not believe in God as well as those who do, often mock rather than celebrate the mysterious nature of true wisdom. But those who met and followed Jesus found in him a wisdom worth longing for.

In some ways, the wisdom that Jesus lived out was not a new idea marketed to the masses. It had been introduced by prophets centuries before. Jesus, of course, was a first-century Jew, who showed special devotion to the Judaism of his ancestors, including its ancient Scriptures. His understanding of wisdom came from studying these Scriptures.

But Jesus also had a special insight all his own about the world, people, life, and God—insight that astonished those around him. The New Testament book of Luke tells of his precocious preoccupation with learning the Scriptures. It tells how once, when Jesus was only a twelve-year-old boy, he and his extended family went with a large group from their hometown to an important Jewish festival in Jerusalem. Tens of thousands of Jews from all over the Mediterranean and Near East attended this festival. Traveling with that kind of entourage would have been a thrill for a small-town boy of twelve, and one that you would think could keep his attention. But after the festival ended, Jesus was off following his own interests, as his parents unwittingly started back home without him.

Mary and Joseph traveled a whole day with the large group that they had come with before realizing that Jesus wasn't with them. As a parent I can only speculate about the nightmare they experienced as they rushed back to find him. I can imagine their frenzy as they looked for their boy throughout the large city of Jerusalem. The city was a crossroads that often saw the likes of slave traders and other unsavory types who might do Jesus harm. Any parent in that circumstance would dread the worst. They looked frantically for two whole days before they finally found him.

What was so riveting to Jesus that he separated from his family and friends? One might think he was spending time in the markets tasting exotic foods that he could never get in his small hometown. Or perhaps he was sitting immersed in the routines of the jugglers, magicians, and other street entertainers who traveled to large festivals like the one in Jerusalem. Yet of all places, Jesus was in the temple talking with the priests and religious leaders, engaging them in conversation and trading questions and answers about the Old Testament and the things of God.

So we shouldn't be surprised when we see in Jesus' life and teachings echos of the ancient Jewish Scriptures about the wisdom of God. Neither should it surprise us that people reacted to his public ministry with a sense of awe over his wisdom.

The Gospel of Mark tells us, "When the Sabbath came, he began to teach in the synagogue, and many who heard him were amazed. 'Where did this man get these things?' they asked. 'What's this wisdom that has been given him!'" (6:2). Matthew tells us that at the end of Jesus' Sermon on the Mount, "the crowds were amazed at his teaching, because he taught as one who had authority, and not as their teachers of the law" (7:28–29). Jesus had fully absorbed and was living out ancient Israel's long-awaited wisdom of God.

The Prophecy of God's Wisdom Fulfilled

No one frames the wisdom of God in the life of Jesus more clearly than St. Paul. In his letter to the church of Corinth, Paul

PARADOXY

answered what were becoming routine questions from Jews and Greeks (Gentiles) alike who were new to Christianity. Previously held beliefs and, no doubt, nagging relatives and friends who had not yet adopted Christianity were confusing Paul's early Christian audiences on a variety of topics. One such topic was, what is real wisdom?

Paul responded,

> For the message of the cross is foolishness to those who are perishing, but to us who are being saved it is the power of God. For it is written:
>
> > "I will destroy the wisdom of the wise;
> > the intelligence of the intelligent I will frustrate."
>
> Where is the wise man? Where is the scholar? Where is the philosopher of this age? Has not God made foolish the wisdom of the world? For since in the wisdom of God the world through its wisdom did not know him, God was pleased through the foolishness of what was preached to save those who believe. Jews demand miraculous signs and Greeks look for wisdom, but we preach Christ crucified: a stumbling block to Jews and foolishness to Gentiles, but to those whom God has called, both Jews and Greeks, Christ the power of God and the wisdom of God.

1 Corinthians 1:18–24

The paradox of God's "foolish wisdom" lies in the reference Paul pulled from the Old Testament prophet, Isaiah: "I will destroy the wisdom of the wise; the intelligence of the intelligent I will frustrate."

Isaiah recounts how God's people self-destructed as they split in civil war; they became absorbed in lives of wealth, power, and unfaithfulness to God, and their hearts fell away from the love relationship they once had with him. Their worship ceremonies became rote and hollow.

Isaiah records the consequence of all this: the destruction of their divided nation by Assyria in 722 BC and Babylon in 586 BC. The armies of these powerful and brutal empires decimated Jerusalem, destroying their fields, killing their kings and leaders, separating their families, and taking most of their few survivors away to live in exile and slavery for years to come.

But Isaiah's story is not without hope and redemption. The book gives cryptic but repeated promises of how God will salvage his people. The key to God's salvation plan, Isaiah says, involves a Redeemer—a Messiah (a chosen or "anointed" one)—who will restore and renew God's people. Through this prophesied one, God's grace will mend the damage to his people and offer not just them but the whole world the promised hope of a new future.

Isaiah's prophesied leader of hope is referred to throughout the book as one who will bring the very wisdom of God. Isaiah 11:1–2 describes him as a royal leader, saying, "A shoot will come up from the stump of Jesse [the royal line]; from his roots a Branch will bear fruit. The Spirit of the Lord will rest on him—the Spirit of wisdom and of understanding." Isaiah 9:6–7 extols the breadth of this Redeemer's emotional, political, spiritual, parental, and divine wisdom saying, "For to us a child is born, to us a son is given, and the government will be on his shoulders. And he will be called Wonderful Counselor, Mighty God, Everlasting Father, Prince of Peace. Of the increase of his government and peace there will be no end."

From this prophetic context Paul further unfolds the oracle in 1 Corinthians 1: the coming of Jesus Christ and his death on

PARADOXY

the cross *is* God's fulfillment of the prophesied Redeemer who offers new hope to a broken world. The pitiable irony, Paul says, is that so many are missing it.

Missing God's Point

Many of Paul's own Jewish compatriots were missing God's real wisdom because they were looking for miraculous signs. Paul was all too familiar with his people's habit of seeking the sensational, believing that miracles would validate those who truly spoke for God. But Paul also knew that sometimes we must watch for God to speak to us in a still small voice (1 Kings 19:11–13), through a damp fleece (Judg. 6:36–40), or through a baby born to insignificant parents on the outer edge of the Roman Empire (Luke 2:1–7). The non-Jewish world, which Paul often referred to in shorthand as "the Greeks," were missing God's wisdom because they too were looking for the wrong thing. Paul recognized the oratorical skill of the Greek philosophers, but their preoccupation was with intellectual advancement alone. Jesus offered far more than miracles and lofty philosophy.

Paul's point was simply this: planet Earth is missing out on God's true wisdom that can be found in the life, work, and death of Jesus because humanity has a persistent tendency to look for spiritual answers in the wrong things, in the wrong places, and with the wrong motives. As a result, we do not find God's real wisdom. We find substitutes that only amount to cheap tricks or prideful self-importance. Aquiring the wisdom of God, Paul said, requires something much more difficult than doing miracles or becoming an accomplished academic.

A Low Door

Very often the best gifts of God come only when we release our grip on our pride. The first fight that my wife, Jan, and I ever had after we married happened when we lived in a small house in Salt Lake City. It was a cold evening and we had planned to stay in for the night. After dinner we began to discuss a topic that I forgot about before our exchange was even over. I remember it wasn't what Jan said that started to annoy me. It was the way she said it. She later told me that she felt the same way.

As we talked, eyebrows furrowed, muscles tensed, and volume increased. Our conversation quickly became less about the topic at hand and more about who could be more sarcastic, clever, and biting with our words. Before either of us knew what was happening, we were yelling at the top of our lungs. I got up from my chair and roared something dramatic like, "Okay, no problem. If that's what you're really like, then I'm outta here!" I stomped to the front door, grabbed a jacket and keys, and pitched open the door. Jan was yelling back something about "Fine, I'm glad!" as I slammed the door behind me so hard that the mailbox fell from the front of the house.

I got in my car and drove around for over an hour that damp night, getting madder and madder. My mind swung into the wild extremes of posttraumatic stream-of-consciousness idiocy. "I'm just gonna leave her, I don't know why I ever married her in the first place anyway, she is going to have to grovel before I ever even consider forgiving her, I'll make sure I get the new TV and couch we just got when I leave. Wait a minute—it's *my* house. *She's* moving out and she can have that stupid cat, I never liked him anyway, but I'M GETTING THE DOG!"

After nearly hitting another car in my nonsensical frenzy, I pulled over and sat in a neighborhood a few blocks from our house. I started to quiet myself. I traced our conversation back in my mind. *She started it*, I thought, and immediately smirked at how juvenile that sounded. I took deep breaths. As I reflected, it occurred to me that Jan might have been right on that first point that I snorted at in sarcasm. And it was my snort that made her react with a re-snort that set me off, which then set her off. I was pretty sure I had started it after all. I couldn't remember much of what else went wrong after that, because the heater in my car wasn't working well and it was getting really cold.

I wanted to go home. Not to my house, to my home. It wasn't getting into my house that was the problem, it was getting back into a right relationship with Jan, and that was home for me. But more than anything else—more than being right (though I still wanted that) and more than hearing her apologize—what I really wanted was to be together with her again.

Now, in all of this I wasn't going to talk to God about it, because I was pretty sure what he would say. Then it hit me, the only way I was going to get back into my home was the same way I have to go to God when I've strayed from him—through that very low door called humility. I winced and swallowed hard. I wasn't sure I was ready to do that. But it was not getting warmer, and it was getting later. And I really didn't like this feeling of separation.

I started the car and headed toward home. I parked and went up to the front door. I picked up the mailbox and rehung it on the house. Then I clicked the lock and slid open the door. Jan was sitting on the couch with a blanket. She didn't speak. Her eyes had a look that I remember well. It was a look of uncertainty that asked me a hundred questions without even speaking: "Are you still mad? Are you a person who is able to make up? Have I married a person who can resolve this kind of conflict with me? How do we do this? I don't like this at all."

I spoke first. "Jan, I was wrong. I shouldn't have talked to you like that, and I'm sorry, honey. Will you forgive me?"

She started to cry and told me how sorry she was too. We got specific about the things we were sorry for, and we hugged each other. Then we went to bed with such passions of forgiveness that I got up the next morning wondering if maybe I ought to get in fights like that more often.

Something serious hit me the next day. It was important to put an imprint early on in our marriage that says, "It is okay if we disagree, even disagree strongly, but only if we can find our way through that low door. It's all right to argue and fight, but only if we have the will to humble ourselves and make up."

We did. We proved it. Since then Jan and I have had other serious arguments from time to time. And sometimes she's had to find her way through that low door of humility. What we both have come to relearn each time, however, is that when you finally find your way through it, it doesn't really hurt at all. In fact, it heals.

A Fool's Paradox

In 1 Corinthians 1, St. Paul says that the problem with human wisdom is that it is so often accompanied by arrogance. God's wisdom is found in humility. The Old Testament affirms this: "When pride comes, then comes disgrace, but with humility comes wisdom" (Prov. 11:2). I learned this in that first argument with Jan. Our insistence on being right brought conflict, but our humility brought peace and restored relationship.

PARADOXY

We often behave similarly with God. We struggle with releasing all that we think we've brought to the table. We wrestle because we think we'll have to give up something, which of course we will. We have to give up our prideful arrogance that says to God with uncertainty, "I'm alright. I can handle this righteousness thing myself. I can figure out the purpose of life without you. And I'm doing well with the human frailty and death issues too. I don't need your help, God. Do you believe me?"

Do we believe ourselves? We do need God's help. And if we can just come to the posts of that low door of humility and see the warmth that awaits us on the other side, we just might have the courage to walk through it and say, "God, I was wrong. I'm sorry. I can't do this alone, I do need your help. Will you help me?"

Paul says, "We preach Christ crucified: a stumbling block to Jews and foolishness to Gentiles, but to those whom God has called, both Jews and Greeks, Christ the power of God and the wisdom of God" (1 Cor. 1:23–24). What people are seeking isn't really found in miraculous signs, even when God does them. Nor are our hearts' real longings satisfied through all of the volumes of academic learning in the world.

St. Paul, one of history's great intellectuals, isn't saying, "Put your intellect aside." He's telling us to put aside the things we cling to as wisdom that will rob us of ultimate peace with God.

The Guiding Power of Wisdom

Having taken those steps of humility to restore our relationship with God, we can now carry the wisdom that Jesus lived out into every arena of life. Jesus' persistent quotes and allusions to the ancient biblical wisdom books like Psalms and Proverbs show how much he treasured God's paradoxes of wisdom in his everyday dealings. Proverbs may be the most explicit Old Testament book about wisdom, and it was no doubt one with which Jesus was deeply familiar.

The first thing that Proverbs teaches is that God's wisdom guides and protects us. "Wisdom calls aloud in the street, . . . 'For the waywardness of the simple will kill them, and the complacency of fools will destroy them; but whoever listens to me will live in safety and be at ease, without fear of harm'" (1:20, 32–33).

Proverbs tells us that trying to learn everything by personal experience is stupid. It's better to learn from the mistakes of others; after all, we can't possibly live long enough to make them all ourselves. Proverbs also calls us to find wisdom by allowing God to pilot our lives. "Trust in the Lord with all your heart and lean not on your own understanding; in all your ways acknowledge him, and he will make your paths straight. Do not be wise in your own eyes; fear the Lord and shun evil" (3:5–7).

Underlying these Old Testament teachings on wisdom is the presumption that living an unexamined life—without wisdom, without God—is extremely dangerous. It's not as if life for the fool is never good. In fact, the Old Testament is clear that it can be exciting and even fulfilling *for a while*. But in time, our own self-destructive time bombs of the company we keep, the thoughts we dwell on, the habits we develop, or the complacency we live in begin to make our lives crumble. Our dissatisfaction and boredom, our fixation on always wanting more, eventually lead to damaging results. But the wisdom of God that we've found in Jesus Christ is there to protect us from ourselves. No doubt we all have experiences that drive home this truth.

We lived on the edge of the Mojave Desert for a few years. Without much other recreation in our relatively small town, I

PARADOXY

bought a motocross dirt bike to ride for fun. I had owned several motorcycles through the years, including dirt bikes, so I was not a novice. Still, I had not lived in the desert before, and I found it hard to understand how serious the dangers were.

I remember going out for long rides, for hours at a time on that motorcycle. The desert was beautiful. Coyotes would stand high on a perch a half mile ahead of me, pausing for a game of cat and mouse. Then they'd run on higher and away up a craggy peak out of my sight.

One day I raced out into the desert where I had not gone before, beyond two or three small mountain ranges. I rode several miles before I came to the top of a vista looking out across the vastness of that sand-covered sea. It was magnificent. Then I turned and looked where I'd come from. It was long, wide, and vast too. The sun was hot and bright. I looked at the cell phone I brought. The heat of the day had nearly drained the battery.

It occurred to me, what would I do if I broke down here? Could I get back? Could I push that heavy bike, and even if I left it, would the small bottle of water I brought be enough for those many miles back home? I turned my bike around, more gently this time than when I came. With a little healthier sense of caution, I clicked first gear with my foot and headed back home. I didn't race; on the way back, I rode.

The next day I was awakened by my clock radio. The news that quietly came from its speakers announced that a man had died the day before in the Mojave Desert, just five miles from my town. The jeep he took into the desert broke down. The five-mile walk in the heat was too much for him; he died of heat exhaustion and dehydration.

We jog down dark alleys of secret living to get a surge of adrenaline, even though we know that those adventures take us far from where we belong, far from the help that we will need when we find trouble. But then we stay too long, and our memory of God's real desires for us to have a truly good life causes us to reflect, then turn around. God's wisdom straightens those crooked, winding paths and lights the way home. His wisdom gives us comfort and rest during the good as well as the bad journeys of life.

Fool's Wisdom

The paradox of "fool's wisdom" is that Jesus didn't come as a bombastic preacher, a brilliant philosopher, with booming trumpets announcing his entrance to each new city. He was born the son of an insignificant family on the outskirts of the empire. He never traveled far from his home. He didn't write books, make films, or hang around with the jet set. Yet the life and work of Jesus has impacted the entire human race, more so than any person who has ever lived.

The cross is the most identifiable symbol to the billions of people who inhabit earth today. And even more important is what it signifies: the possibility of experiencing divine forgiveness for anyone who will trust Jesus for it, and the symbol of ultimate love and self-sacrifice that is the standard for the best and deepest kinds of relationships.

We chase after things that we hope will help us find a true home, but instead, lead us to a dead end. The paradox of God's foolish wisdom seen in Jesus' life and death can help us find our way. What truly quenches our hearts' deepest longings is, first of all, to be in a right relationship with the one who loves us most, the God of the universe; and second, to live out in all areas of life the humility that helped us find our way back to God. That's real wisdom. That's the foolish wisdom of God.

Jesus' death on the cross on behalf of humanity makes real wisdom available to us, because it makes divine forgiveness possible. Finding the wisdom of God relieves us of the cleverness that we think we need to impress God, others, and even ourselves. It allows us to exist without the constant fear that we must somehow live miraculously righteous lives or lives of ingenious insight. When we accept that, we find that we can return from those ill-considered trips and find our way through those low doors of restored relationships. It doesn't hurt after all. It heals.

Meditation

God grant me the serenity
To accept the things I cannot change,
The courage to change the things I can,
And the wisdom to know one from the other.

Reinhold Niebuhr (1892–1971)

7: The Power of Positive Weakness
Yield to Conquer

Therefore, whoever humbles himself like this child is the greatest in the kingdom of heaven.

Jesus

When I am weak, then I am strong.

St. Paul

Toulon, Illinois, was one of the innumerable small towns that dotted the vast corn, soybean, and wheat fields on the gentle rolling plains of the Midwest near the place where I grew up. Most of its residents went no further in their education than high school. Like so many of its counterparts in April 2002, Toulon was a town of peaceable residents, with one notable exception. Curt Thompson, according to a central Illinois newspaper, had earned a reputation for being a town bully. He was a late-middle-aged man with unkempt hair and a history of court appearances, mostly resulting from some feuds with neighbors. Town residents had warned local police that Thompson was potentially violent. But authorities were not prepared for what he did at the home of a young couple and their ten-year-old daughter.

Early one Friday evening, Curt Thompson entered the home of James and Janet Geisenhagen and opened fire on them with a shotgun. Thompson first gunned down the mother, Janet. Hearing the attack, her husband, Jim, ran up the stairs from the basement. Thompson met him with a shotgun blast that sent him tumbling back down.

The Geisenhagen's ten-year-old daughter, Ashley, reportedly knew that her father was dead when his body fell back down the stairs. But undeterred, Ashley ran up to be with her mother who lay alone and critically wounded but still conscious.

Thompson fled the house. Ashley telephoned her grandmother and then her pastor, both of whom arrived before police or paramedics. Ashley's grandmother later reported that the three knelt praying together that Mommy would come through and Daddy would be all right with Jesus.

The mother, Janet, however, died shortly after. The entire incident began with a dispute over a dog bite that escalated to the point where Jim Geisenhagen installed a security camera to videotape Thompson's drive-by stalking episodes near their home.

The story was bewildering. Yet one aspect of the newspaper article was conspicuously clear—the faith of the entire Geisenhagen family. In particular, ten-year-old daughter Ashley revealed astonishing charity, faithfulness to God, and even compassion for her parents' killer.

Ashley's grandmother related that when Ashley had seen Thompson glaring at their house, Ashley said she felt sorry for him because she thought no one loved him. Comforting her be-reaved grandmother, the little girl said, "It's OK, Gramma. We know they [her mom and dad] are in Heaven with Jesus. And if Curt Thompson goes to jail, I'll take my Bible over and read him Scriptures. . . . Gramma, we need to pray for him."[1]

What empowered this ten-year-old child to display that kind of personal strength and graciousness toward such a despicable man? I suspect that her parents and grandmother had greatly influenced her, even as her father had installed the camera with hopes of bringing Thompson to justice. But Ashley's arresting statement of grace toward her family's assailant surely came from something that she herself had become—a person of strong love and strange peace, fashioned by God's grace.

Ashley's spiritual muscle is a penetrating reminder of what happens when a person truly internalizes Jesus' core directives, such as "Love your enemies and pray for those who persecute you" and "Unless you change and become like children, you will never enter the kingdom of heaven" (Matt. 5:44; 18:3).

The Strength of Childlike Trust

What did Jesus mean by his statement about children and the kingdom? After all, "unless you change and become like children, you will never enter the kingdom of heaven" seems like a strong ultimatum. What qualities do children possess that make them superior to the adult disciples to whom Jesus was speaking in the New Testament?

Children trust more easily and deeply than adults. Blind trust? At times, yes, and that is something that most of us do *not* associate with healthy religious faith. But I suspect Jesus was referring to

THE POWER OF POSITIVE WEAKNESS

how children typically trust those whom they love and, perhaps more significantly, those who love them.

When my first son, Aaron, was a toddler, I rediscovered the pleasure of looking unswervingly into another human's eyes again. I had done this as a child. But somewhere along life's way, I became saddled with doubts about whether people liked me, whether they were happy with me, or whether they were uncomfortable with me if I stared into their eyes. I learned, as most of us do, that too long a gaze into someone's eyes can be more than uncomfortable. It can also convey messages: "I'm threatening you," or "I'm thinking romantically about you," or "I think you're strange." Any perceived meaning can elicit a response from the other person, sometimes one that we might not like. They may threaten us back, reject us, or take offense. And so we learn as adults to avoid eye contact that lasts too long.

There I was at home with my little curly-haired, strawberry-blond boy, Aaron. He would come to me and say, "Hi, Daddy," and then look penetratingly into my eyes for as long as he liked. I would look right back, because there was absolutely no reason to avert my eyes. It was wonderful and healing.

But the strength to engage our eyes came from Aaron, not me. I responded only when he initiated that wonderful little dance of our hearts that I came to love. He could do that because, when children trust those who love them, their relationships are not based on competition. Sure, they still race Dad to the car or try to beat Grandpa at checkers. But those things are done in a spirit of fun and playfulness. They are ways to enjoy those relationships more, with laughter and learning.

That kind of play is not the same as the kind of competition that develops in the adult world—where the businesswoman tries to gain the upper hand by using inside trading information to buy

PARADOXY

stocks, the college student tries to impress the professor by destroying another student's project, the rising-star athlete takes steroids to win as many races as possible. It doesn't matter to success-driven people that these conquests result in hollow victories. They win the momentary battle of getting ahead but lose the war of maintaining fairness or remaining a person of integrity.

And so Jesus touted children as a model when gaining something so great as the kingdom of heaven, because just as children trust those who love them, Jesus called us to trust God in both the journey and the outcome of our lives. We plan as we need to and set the courses we believe God wants us to take. But after that, we are strongest, Jesus urges, when we accept what we cannot control about the journey and destination.

When circumstances befall us that we never anticipated—and they will—we are strongest when we trust God. When that unexpected layoff comes, a loved one dies, that university rejects us; when we don't get the part in the production, our friends fail us, or our investments tank, we find our greatest power in that place of quiet trust in the presence of God, that place where we listen for God's voice.

"Be still, and know that I am God," the Old Testament says (Ps. 46:10). Yet stillness before God is as uncomfortable for many as looking someone in the eyes for a long time. We learn to do it only as we experience life and become convinced that God truly loves us.

Jesus suggests this is a cornerstone of our relationship with God. We find our greatest strength when we trust like children do, with that innocent but resilient and flexible trust. When we do that, we pray through the toughest circumstances.

A few years ago I went through some of the most painful circumstances I had ever experienced. It involved my work as a minister at a church—a place where you'd hope people treat each other well. Regrettably, that was not the case. The details aren't important; those who have suffered negative work experiences understand the deep pain that I am talking about.

As often happens in human organizations, sacred and secular, a few wanted power over the many. I resisted. Passion and egos, including mine, swung wildly and calculatedly in all directions, aiming to lacerate one another and hitting their targets most of the time.

As the years have passed, the soreness of that time is fading, but the memory of how God got me through those circumstances hangs like a gorgeous sunset in a rearview mirror. Though I went through months of deep sadness and discouragement at a time, I remember how much more I came to trust God through it all. After begging God to change my circumstances and stop the pain, I prayed, "God, I hate my life right now. But I know you love me and that gives me hope. I know you see my circumstances in ways that I can't. I trust you to keep your hand on the throttle of how much I can take. Give me the grace to get through today. Maybe someday you could show me how you're going to use this to better me. Until then, I know that I can trust you for peace, even in times like these."

When we trust like children as Jesus directs, we gain an unexpected strength. We learn to say with St. Paul, "If God is for us, who can be against us?" (Rom. 8:31). God has our best interests at heart and can see us through all of life's assaults.

The Strength of Childlike Weakness

As children we long to grow up. "I'm *not* just five, I'm five and a half!" the little girl insists. Her assertion clearly reveals

PARADOXY

her underlying belief that growing up will make her even better than she is now. In her heart, she knows that she doesn't have all the strength, skills, knowledge, training, or power that she needs or wants. But she will when she's big, she thinks to herself. Her mom tells a friend in the little girl's presence, "Yep, she's really looking forward to her next birthday." And her little girl beams with a smile. The child is a walking admission that she has weaknesses—areas of her life that limit her, with which she needs help, and which at times may even pain her.

Children want to grow strong. Their knowledge of their own helplessness is not bad. It is not based on some neurotic lack of development or personal deficiency. It is normal. Children play games imitating what they want to become—astronaut, doctor, mommy, superhero, teacher, fireman, actor. In playing those roles, they recognize that in reality they are not yet there. Still, they continue to dream that someday they will possess the power to become what they want to be.

St. Paul advocated Jesus' principle of childlike weakness that can give people of all ages the strength and hope to face life's toughest situations. Paul uses children as a positive model for the truly spiritual person. In his letter to the Christians at Rome he wrote,

> The true children of God are those who let God's Spirit lead them. The Spirit that we received is not a spirit that makes us slaves again to fear. The Spirit that we have makes us children of God. . . . If we are God's children, then we will receive the blessings God has for us.
>
> Romans 8:14–15a, 17 ICB

At other times, however, Paul referred to children as a negative model of what adults should be. He wrote to the Christians at the church he established at Corinth, "Brothers and sisters, do not be children in your thinking; rather, be infants in evil, but in thinking be adults" (1 Cor. 14:20 NRSV); and a few verses earlier, "When I was a child, I talked like a child, I thought like a child, I reasoned like a child. When I became a man, I put childish ways behind me"

Paul's teaching does not contradict itself. It is simply a difference that we still make today between *childish* and *childlike*. Childish behavior is selfish, juvenile, and naive. A childlike attitude, on the other hand, is innocent, dependent, and guileless. Being childlike is an attribute of Jesus' true disciples. It's in our childlike dependence on God that we find God's strength for living.

The Pain of Admitting Our Weaknesses

Making the leap from living with my struggles and weaknesses to acknowledging my need for God's help to cope with them is rarely easy. I would rather concentrate on the origins, size, or extent of my personal problems, which paralyzes rather than energizes me toward change.

"Why am I going through this, God?" "Why have you given me this condition?" "Why have you put me in these circumstances?" "Why do I have so many limitations?" I have asked God those questions, sometimes in quiet personal agony and sometimes in furious anger. I have cried out to the Lord, incensed at what seems to be God's careless neglect of my situation. I have known the frustration of beating on the thick, brass doors of heaven, with no apparent answer. I would add that I have never felt guilty about approaching God in those moments of pain. God can take it and is even touched by my honesty.

PARADOXY

Jesus was no stranger to prayers of anguish. Prior to his crucifixion, Jesus prayed in a garden called Gethsemane on the Mount of Olives, just east of the city of Jerusalem. Knowing that he was about to experience abandonment and an excruciating torture and then death, at one point he seemed nearly desperate to veer from the mission that would place him in the hands of those conspiring to kill him. He prayed, "Father, if you are willing, take this cup from me; yet not my will, but yours be done" (Luke 22:42). Three New Testament books record this prayer in which Jesus called out to God to rescue him from this onslaught. And all three record Jesus' submission to his Father's will. In yielding his will to God's, Jesus found the strength to face crucifixion, which the Bible later describes as cosmically essential for the salvation of humanity.

St. Paul also admitted having crippling personal weaknesses but said that in acknowledging them before God and looking to God for strength, he found spiritual and personal power. Paul wrote,

> So a painful problem was given to me. This problem is a messenger from Satan. It is sent to beat me and keep me from being too proud. I begged the Lord three times to take this problem away from me. But the Lord said to me, "My grace is enough for you. When you are weak, then my power is made perfect in you." So I am very happy to brag about my weaknesses. Then Christ's power can live in me. . . . And I am happy, because when I am weak, then I am truly strong.
>
> 2 Corinthians 12:7b–10 ICB

Our trials, tears, and trouble are often what God uses so powerfully to remove our prideful ambitions, our selfish pursuits, our indifference toward God—the things he knows will hurt us. But pain is not always for that purpose. Paul shows that we don't have to pretend that our agonies aren't real. In fact, it is smack dab in the middle of them that we can cry out to God, as Jesus and Paul did. Even when we learn how powerfully God uses our misfortunes, it's not necessary for us to pretend they are good.

I have a dear friend who suffers with a debilitating physical condition that causes severe pain in her joints and extreme exhaustion. It has attacked her vital organs over the years. A brilliant academic, she related to me a discussion she had with some of her Yale University colleagues about the topic of suffering. During the discussion, a graduate student who appeared to be trying to impress everyone began to poetically praise pain as one of God's great tools.

With gracious calm my friend spoke. "You know," she said, "I'd like to insist that we not do something here. Let's not glorify suffering. I have lived for many years with an illness that may one day take my life. Until then, it is sure to cause me untold days of pain. I know probably better than most of you what suffering is like and that God can do good things in me in spite of it. But don't confuse the suffering itself with the goodness and preciousness of God who saves me in the midst of it."

It is not weakness that is wonderful; it is God's gracious gifts in the middle of our powerlessness. Our frailty is simply the lens that allows us to see the goodness of the gifts and the Giver clearly. Whether we're suffering in some aspect of our weakness or reveling in whatever strength God gives us, he meets us in either place, delighted when we draw close.

We are often not properly awed when we see God in our strength. When we feel strong, we think we don't need God; but this should be a warning sign. Our strengths often create our

PARADOXY

greatest downfalls. The successful politician uses his charisma to seduce the young woman, rather than work for justice as he originally intended. The televangelist uses his gift of public speaking to cajole excessive amounts of money from his viewers. Many of them need his good words of encouragement, but they can hardly afford to give anything more from their meager Social Security checks. In those instances, it is almost as though we mistake our human, moral frailties for strength.

In Mark 12:30, Jesus says, "Love the Lord your God . . . with all your strength." It's interesting that the only thing that Jesus actually asks us to do with true strength, once we have it, is to love God. But in our weak times, our need for God becomes clearer. I heard a preacher say once, "God uses broken things. Broken soil to produce a crop, broken clouds to give rain, broken grain to give bread, broken bread to give strength." Jesus portrayed his own life as a piece of broken bread at his last supper with his disciples just before he was crucified. After breaking bread before them, Jesus said, "This is my body given for you" (Luke 22:19). The confidence of knowing your strengths—based on your talents, gifts, and skills—is a good thing. But having the ability to admit your shortcomings before God and others is even better. Ironically, it is when we come clean with our weaknesses and afflictions before God that he reveals to us indescribable divine strength, faithfulness, and comfort.

The Healing of Admitting Our Weaknesses

I often think that owning up to our weaknesses would be easier if we could see some advantage in it. When we presume that we have so much to lose—our pride, our power, our reputations, our advantage over others—we see only the reasons *not* to be honest anything less than our ideal. Yet when we truly believe that the outcome of fessing up to our limitations, inadequacies, and afflictions will net positive results, we are more likely to disclose who we really are to God and others. The New Testament author, James, recognized this: "Confess your sins to each other and pray for each other so that you may be healed" (James 5:16).

Life's best seems to be reserved for those who, at some point and with some trusted friend, open up in penetratingly honest self-disclosure. When we confess, we shake off those neck-breaking, weighty masks that we hold to our faces so that no one will know the real us. We liberate ourselves from getting up each day and putting on the time-consuming makeup of pretend personas and unrealistic achievements that we want others to believe about us. When we admit our weaknesses, neither in arrogant defiance nor in undue shame, but rather in simple naked confession, we find ourselves truly free to accept God's forgiveness and strength.

But how is that so? How does God use that open, childlike, honest living to our advantage?

Admitting Weakness Relieves Us

First, in blatant honesty we are free to rely on God rather than exclusively on our own power. How refreshing to breathe deeply and relax in the admission that God is stronger than we are. He is ready and able to carry our heaviest burdens.

St. Paul vividly communicates this principle of Jesus when he talks about how he took one of his most serious and nagging life problems to God over and over in prayer. He does not tell

PARADOXY

us what the problem is, clearly because God's answer is more important than his problem. But Paul tells us that God finally unwound his stress in an answer to his prayers that said, "My grace is sufficient for you."

Now this answer is not the same as the ever unsatisfying answer of the exhausted parent who tells the persistent child, "Shut up. You'll take what I give you and like it!" No, God is telling Paul, "*My* grace (and not your efforts or strength) are sufficient to combat your problem. You'll get through this, Paul. And you don't even have to rely on your own strength. I'll supply grace in your emotions, your circumstances, through loving friends, and in ways you never imagined, so that you can conquer that personal weakness that I know you're struggling with. So just trust me with it and relax." God promises to be there with us. And that is sufficient.

Admitting Weakness Matures Us

Second, God uses our admission of weakness to mature us. St. Paul tells us that God further answered his prayers to take away his weakness by telling him, "My grace is sufficient for you, *for my power is made perfect in weakness*" (2 Cor. 12:9, emphasis added). Jesus' principle of yielding to God to find victory in God's strength is a process—a process that is intended to fulfill and complete our humanness.

The original New Testament Greek word for "perfect" in God's answer to Paul is *teleios*, from which we derive our word "telescope." It implies an achievement, a looking from the now to the future, where we become more complete. It implies a maturing that takes place in those who acknowledge that God has superior

THE POWER OF POSITIVE WEAKNESS

and everlasting strength. Recognizing our frailties is essential to the process of spiritual maturity.

I have heard that in the Swiss Alps there is a sort of shrine to honor a mountain guide who gave his life while ascending a peak to save a stranded, desperate tourist. On the memorial is inscribed "He died climbing." Maturing people always seem to have that notion in their hearts. Their real successes come in surrendering their lives to God's purposes for them. They ascend in strength and character when they sacrifice for the sake of others.

In Philippians, St. Paul portrays how his process of yielding his life resulted in a simultaneous awareness that he was headed toward spiritual maturity, even though he always knew that he had not yet arrived. His constant admission that he did not have it all together entwined beautifully with his maturing process that came as God infused Paul with strength. He writes,

> Not that I have already obtained this or have already reached the goal; but I press on to make it my own, because Christ Jesus has made me his own. Beloved, I do not consider that I have made it my own; but this one thing I do: forgetting what lies behind and straining forward to what lies ahead, I press on toward the goal for the prize of the heavenly call of God in Christ Jesus. Let those of us then who are mature be of the same mind; and if you think differently about anything, this too God will reveal to you.
>
> Philippians 3:12–15 NRSV

Paul looks like an effortless runner in this passage. He knows that he belongs in the family of Jesus Christ. His confidence comes from his trust that God will reveal anything to him that he needs to understand. He has come to know God's purposes that propel

PARADOXY

his life. Paul's life reveals a key mark of spiritual maturity—the calm assurance that God is in control.

Admitting Weakness Deepens Us

God uses our weaknesses to deepen us. Being a deep person is different from being a mature person. I have met people whom I consider mature but who do not necessarily strike me as deep.

Deep people generally seem to handle things well like mature people do, but they also have broad life experience and profound empathy toward the tragedies and difficulties of others. Deep people have a full understanding of life. They are comfortable in their own skin, warts and all. They have learned to live with the contradictions and tensions that exist in life.

Deep people have almost always journeyed down experiential and internal caverns of the heart, exploring pain and doubts about everything from God to self. Many have experienced some kind of personal suffering and yet have made peace with that. They have come back out into the sunshine of living with the quiet confidence that they do not need to be certain of everything in order to live well.

God is with us in our trials to accomplish his purposes. A story is told about a man who had to cross a wide river on the ice. He was afraid it might be too thin, so he began to crawl on his hands and knees in great terror. He thought he might fall through at any moment. Just as he neared the opposite shore, exhausted, another man glided past him nonchalantly, sitting on a sled pulled by dogs and loaded with iron. We are so often like the man crawling on the ice. We tremble every step of the way through difficult periods of life as though God's promises might give way underneath us.

So how do we yield to God's strength over ours, so that we have the confidence that God will sustain us no matter what? How do we find God's power by surrendering and admitting that our strength alone just won't do? How do we learn to lean on God? First, we must examine our single greatest roadblock in turning to God.

The Essence of Sin

I have heard many Christians simplistically say that *sin* stands between us and God. This reminds me of the time I asked my father how a special effect was done in an action movie we were watching together. He glibly replied, "Trick photography." I was looking for something more.

Of course, sin is the part of the human condition that the Bible says lies at the root of what distances us from God and from one another. But what is sin, really?

From the beginning of the Bible in Genesis, the human experience as described in the Garden of Eden narrative revolves around the "tree of the knowledge of good and evil." That tree epitomizes God's message to humans: "You can have power and stewardship over nearly everything else in your world—plants, animals, sea creatures, your own bodies—but when it comes to that morality stuff, don't mess with that. It'll kill you. Trust my lead on that one."

As the narrative goes, despite God's warnings, disaster strikes when man and woman take initiative in Genesis 3 to control their own moral and spiritual destinies rather than obey God. Adam and Eve eat of the forbidden tree, God confronts them about it, they play the blame game, and God banishes them from the

PARADOXY

garden because they seriously damaged their relationship with the Creator. It ends with their eventual death.

Just after Adam and Eve have eaten of the tree, God confronts them for what they've done. Adam and Eve are hiding, ashamed because they are naked. God asks, "Who told you that you were naked? Have you eaten from the tree I told you not to?!" (see Gen. 3:11). Many commentators have read that as a prosecutor's interrogation. But I think it can be read another way. God is inviting them to confess. Like a loving parent, God is trying to see if they will reenter their now broken relationship with him and with one another. To be sure, God thought that they had done wrong. But he was more interested in the possibility of a renewed relationship than in the satisfaction of placing blame.

The focal point of the violation was that up until that point, humans had been in a wonderful relationship of complete and utter trust with God. They had walked together in the garden, talked about the wonders of the creation, and enjoyed one another's company beyond measure. But when they chose to partake of the tree of knowledge of good and evil, they said in effect that they wanted to usurp God's role, which provided them with moral and spiritual protection. The possibility of being more powerful than God was better than the pleasure of peaceful relations all around. Their violation was about trust and power.

Many of the characters in the Bible misunderstand the true nature of sin again and again. Humans repeatedly tend to think that sin is a set of broken rules. However, Genesis 3 shows us that the problem is not really about rules but what sin does to how we think about ourselves and God. Sin is the two-beat process of first mistrusting God and then idolizing anything above our love relationship with God.

THE POWER OF POSITIVE WEAKNESS

Mother Teresa of Calcutta said,

Our intellect and other gifts have been given to be used for God's greater glory, but sometimes they become the very god for us. That is the saddest part; we are losing our balance when this happens. We must [empty] ourselves to be filled by God. Even God cannot fill what is full.[2]

In Genesis 3, sin is turning away and not trusting God. We can keep all the rules and still sin because we don't trust God. That's the real essence of sin.

Leaning on God

All of this leads us to the crux of Jesus' paradox about yielding to become like children. There is genuine power available to those who will freely acknowledge their shortcomings, trust God with wild abandon, and learn to revel in a renewed relationship with their Designer. But how do we yield in order to conquer our selfish nature?

First, people who yield their lives to acquire God's daily strength do so by choice. This deliberate surrender takes different shapes. For some, that trade of power may occur every week in the quiet of their hearts in a church during the Eucharist. For others, it may be in a public testimony among other trusted Christian friends and worshipers. For still others it may happen in a bar, in a moment of despair when life has not turned out as they hoped. At the end of their rope, they mumble a prayer in desperation, "I give up, God! You win. I've tried to do everything my way. My failures outweigh my successes. Take my life. I want to follow you. Make the most of what I have left." Whatever form

PARADOXY

it takes, becoming like a child before God as Jesus told us to do is not something that occurs by accident.

Those who learn to yield their strength to God have also learned to be humble. It is hard to resist the urge to demand credit and seek adulation. One of the most striking people described in the Bible was John the Baptist. This prophet-vagabond who preceded Jesus gained a considerable following and some celebrity during his life. Josephus, the renowned Jewish historian, reported many years after John's death that people still trembled at the thought of him. Jesus made a public tribute to John, saying, "Among those born of women there has not risen anyone greater than John the Baptist" (Matt. 11:11).

Despite any reputation John may have built for himself, when he prophesied about Jesus and recognized him as the predicted Messiah, the anointed one whom the Jewish people were awaiting, John said, "I am not worthy to stoop down and untie the thong of his sandals" (Mark 1:7 NRSV). And after Jesus came onto the scene and throngs of people began to swarm to Jesus instead of John, some observers publicly asked John about this. His response was simply, "He must increase, but I must decrease" (John 3:30 NRSV).

Instead of giving a speech about all he had done to pave the way for Jesus, John simply bowed out, recognizing that he did what God had called him to do. He knew he would not find any strength or advantage in grandstanding about it. Another time, when people asked John who he was, he simply indicated, "I am nobody. I am to be heard, not to be seen. I am just a voice" (see John 1:19–23).

This kind of humility was true of every biblical figure who changed the world. Moses recorded his failures as well as his accomplishments. The Bible recounts his uncontrollable rage, impatience, lack of trust in God, and his fear to face new situations. King David wrote many of the Psalms, yet he did not brag about his victory over Goliath or his other military exploits. Solomon's Ecclesiastes doesn't boast about his brilliance in setting up an exemplary kingdom and system of justice that even the queen of Sheba came to see. No, biblical figures were painfully human. Their greatness often came in spite of who they were. They did not draw undue attention to themselves.

We live in an age of "bests"—the best actor, best movie, best contestant, best . . . you fill in the blank. High school juniors were polled recently about where they thought they'd be in five years. A large majority said they planned to be presidents and CEOs of companies, leading actors, and multimillionaires. But what about the relief worker who helps hundreds of thousands escape an African famine or an Asian AIDS crisis? The teacher who spends a lifetime educating poor kids at an urban grade school? Or the attorney who regularly gives up several of her high-priced hours per week to give justice to people who could not otherwise dream of getting it?

We chase after position, power, and titles. We want people to recognize our achievements and address us properly. No wonder we cannot be filled with God's strength. We are stuffed so full of ourselves that Jesus Christ cannot be seen in us. Jesus calls you and me to humility. That's precisely when God calls us to yield to his will like children so that he can fill our lives with divine power.

Finally, those who yield to God's ways don't presume to have a corner on his mind. The most annoying religious believers I have been around, of any faith, are those who presume to have an exclusive copy of God's script for their lives, and the lives of others, in their hands. They pontificate with surgical certainty about who is in with God and who is out. They preach about what real righteousness is. They wag their fingers at popular culture, detailing what, when, and how God will deal with our

PARADOXY

wicked world and our failed organized religious and humanitarian endeavors. All this is done in an effort to prove that they have gotten to know God so well that they now speak exclusively for him. What presumption.

Biblical prophets who spoke for God were commonly reluctant to do it. They recognized what a dicey matter it is to claim to talk for God or speak with certainty about judgment, success, or the future.

The New Testament book of James puts it this way:

> Some of you say, "Today or tomorrow we will go to some city. We will stay there a year, do business, and make money." But you do not know what will happen tomorrow! Your life is like a mist. You can see it for a short time, but then it goes away. So you should say, "If the Lord wants, we will live and do this or that." But now you are proud and you brag. All of this bragging is wrong."
>
> James 4:13–16 ICB

I have heard it noted that if we brag about our money, homes, or education, they do not diminish in value. But when we brag about our spiritual accomplishments, they will evaporate like steam.

Those of us who choose to yield our will to God live in the tension between longing to know his desires for us and never presuming that we have harnessed the mind of God. We live with both the longing for his guidance and the anticipation of his spontaneity.

Hearing God in the Hurricane

There is something about human limitations, pain, and life's troubles that is loud. Not loud in the physical sense of noise, but in the spiritual sense that sound deafens us to God's voice when we need to hear it the most. Life's storms can make God's voice seem faint, and this can make yielding difficult.

One of the early Old Testament prophets, Elijah, learned this lesson in a vivid encounter with God. He was distressed that God's people were in a time of deep disobedience, ignoring God's desires for them. Jezebel, the queen of Israel at the time, was even chasing Elijah to kill him.

Far out in the wilderness, Elijah bemoaned his life's vocation as pointless. He was running for his life, exhausted. While hiding out in a cave, he called out to God for help, to find meaning in his misery. God directed Elijah to come outside. First Kings 19:11b–12 (KJV) describes what awaited him:

> A great and strong wind rent the mountains, and brake in pieces the rocks before the LORD; but the LORD was not in the wind: and after the wind an earthquake; but the LORD was not in the earthquake: and after the earthquake a fire; but the LORD was not in the fire: and after the fire a still small voice.

Elijah had a talk with God. That talk, 1 Kings 19 tells us, gave Elijah strength, direction, meaning, and comfort in all that he was going through. God's instructions for Elijah led to a new chapter for him and for God's people. But before he could experience renewal, Elijah needed to realize that God was not to be found or heard in the sensational, the noisy, or the frenzied of the world, but in the quiet. God came in that "still small voice."

I very much identify with the imagery that Elijah experienced. The whirlwind of my daily business distances me from God. I can be far from the Lord almost without noticing it, pushed by events that seem seismic but end up being of little consequence.

PARADOXY

And the searing heat of life's fires takes so much of my attention that my days pass quickly and years go by before I look up to notice that suddenly it's quiet . . . and there is God.

Jesus went to quiet places to get away from the crowds to pray alone with God. He found God's voice clearest there. I have often found that too. Sometimes God's quiet voice comes to me in a hushed conversation with someone who needs to talk about a struggle he or she is facing; and as I take the time to listen, I find myself hearing God's whisper as well. Sometimes it's in those dawning hours when I first wake, and God speaks to me so gently, bringing things to my mind with an unmatched clarity of thought.

King David of ancient Israel had a life of triumph as well as tragedy. Old Testament narratives tell how he soared to the heights of celebrity when he trounced Goliath and fended off an invading army of Philistines from Israel. David also knew the lonely hours of failure and heartache. After he was caught in adultery, his country fell into civil war, and his own son died while trying to overthrow him. At the end of King David's life, he reconciled all with God and prayed, "Your gentleness has made me great" (2 Sam. 22:36 NKJV). Other translations describe God's posture toward David as "stooping down."

The irony of God's strength is his quiet gentleness. St. Francis of Sales (1567–1622) said, "Nothing is so strong as gentleness; nothing so gentle as real strength." We dare not miss that, because only when we hear God's gentle voice can we tap into the power of the kingdom of heaven that Jesus said comes only to those who are like children. No power on earth can conquer like the Spirit of God within us can. It is the inner, indomitable power that we as humans were always meant to be in touch with. It's the power that supplies us with the strength to overcome what we thought would be our most overwhelming disadvantages.

Meditation

So let it be in God's own might
We gird us for the coming fight,
And, strong in God whose cause is ours,
In conflict with unholy powers,
We grasp the weapons God has given,
The light and truth and love of Heaven.

John Greenleaf Whittier (1807–1892)

PARADOXY

8: Taller When We Bow
Serve to Reign

Whoever wishes to become great among you must be your servant, and whoever wishes to be first among you must be slave of all.

Jesus

I figured that if I said it enough, I would convince the world that I really was the greatest.

Muhammad Ali

Some of the kids in the neighborhood where I grew up sat on the sidewalk in worn thrift-store clothes with their elbows on their knees; others stood in the gutter of the street with one foot on the curb and one hand on their hip. They listened in rapt attention as a boy we called "Goat" told us about his recent exploits at the Gift Avenue Home—a juvenile detention center for delinquent adolescents. Goat was one of several older boys who were self-appointed and acknowledged leaders in our neighborhood. He was tough, cocky, funny, always ready for a fight, and seemed pretty clever. But he was not clever enough to avoid being sent to the Gift Home.

Goat had just returned from Gift after getting caught robbing a local Burger King. He drank beer from a can wrapped in a paper bag as he told us about how tough kids at Gift had constantly looked to fight him or steal the few things Goat had taken with him. But he had kept a low profile and managed to avoid more trouble.

Goat made us laugh as he'd break the tension of his otherwise harrowing stories by mocking how the guardians at Gift sounded when they got the teenage detainees up at 6:00 a.m. to oversee the inmate kids' day. He swaggered and laughed as though none of it had really fazed him. But later, my close boyhood friends and I agreed in private that deep down it bothered him.

Goat's stories about Gift Home were pretty intense, though we suspected they were true. They were very similar to those that other older boys had told us when they either returned or "escaped" after the juvenile courts sent them there.

There was a sort of disturbing progression in my neighborhood. First, when you were caught for your crimes—usually robbery, vandalism, or dealing drugs—you were first sent to Gift Home for a stint. If you persisted, which many of the kids in our area did, you were sent to the legendary facility in St. Charles, Illinois—a dreaded place with reported initiations of sexual assault or physical beatings. If you still didn't straighten out by your age of majority, you'd end up at the big house, the state penitentiary in Joliet.

I never sensed that the kids in our neighborhood *wanted* to go to any of those places. Some of them, however, seemed to have

PARADOXY

little chance to do better, given the horrible family situations they came from. Their fathers and older siblings, to the extent they knew them, had followed that sad itinerary, so why not them? Others started into a life of crime to find excitement and to escape the boredom of having so little. In no time they went from being a cute feisty kid to a mug shot at juvenile hall. Who knows the number of miles they walked down those indifferent corridors of state justice.

Sometimes I don't know how my brother and I found our way out of the maze. But we did. Raised below the poverty line during our childhood years, we both managed to graduate from great universities with multiple graduate degrees and good jobs. I'm not bragging. I'm relieved and thankful.

I often think back on the years in our old neighborhood. What made my brother and me, and the other few who dodged those pitfalls, different? For me the answers were a few models of true leadership, some dreams of greatness, and a God who entered my life again and again, offering grace where I hadn't earned it and mercy where I didn't deserve it.

Admittedly, my dreams were not initially mine. They were sparked by those who were leaders in my life, though I often didn't acknowledge them as such. Our parents, some relatives, and close family friends loved us and served as our leaders; they were unwilling to let my brother and me simply do as we pleased. They prayed for us continually. They instilled hope in us that life could be better, that we could be better.

I have often wondered if some of my childhood friends, who by their mid to late teens ended up pregnant and on welfare, or in the penal system, or even dead, ever had leaders to offer them dreams of greatness. Did they ever see models of hope or realistic ideals of improvement? Did a mom or dad, a relative or friend ever help them see that there was something beyond the broken, red-brick streets in front of our houses? I hope so. In fact, I still hope so. If they are still living, and even if their lives saw early disappointments, I have often hoped and prayed that somewhere along the way someone showed them glimpses of hope, no matter what their pasts.

Jesus gave and still gives people those hopes. It is neither through our might nor cleverness that it comes about. Like Jesus' other teachings, true greatness comes about, not when we shout loud or long enough about how great we are, but when we stoop to become servants.

What the World Wants

Greatness is a relevant topic for everyone I have ever known. Emotionally and mentally, healthy people desire at least *some* kind of greatness. We want to be great athletes, moms, artists, students, or lovers. We want to be great at our jobs, our financial investments, our hobbies, or our religious and intellectual pursuits. We want great friends, great places to live, great vacations, and great memories. And even with those who seem to seek no aspects of greatness at all, a deeper look reveals that they still desire things like great solitude or great humility.

Our individual ideas of greatness are determined, for the most part, by the quality of the leadership that influences our lives. Many automatically presume that the word *leader* signifies a person in some grand position who can brilliantly direct a group of people to do wonderful things. Many people are content to be followers, so they assume that leadership is not for them. But this thinking is mistaken. The father of a little

PARADOXY

boy is a leader, whether or not he sees himself in that role. That little boy may be a leader at his school when he tells his two playmates that he doesn't want to talk crudely about or beat up another kid.

We also assume that a leader's greatness is relative to the size of his following or undertaking. But this thinking also misconstrues ideas of leadership. The greatest leaders may lead very small groups or seemingly insignificant causes. Conversely, dozens of the world's most appalling and infamous dictators have led armies of hundreds of thousands to destroy the destinies of millions.

Leadership may be brief, or it may be long term. It may involve thousands of complicated decisions, or it may occur in the single quiet moment of what a person elects *not* to do. Leadership may be very tangible, or it may be quite abstract. And to the shock of many, leadership may be voluntary or involuntary.

People are watching us whether we realize it or not. I remember an interview with a professional basketball player who had gotten into legal and ethical trouble some years ago. Parents criticized him, saying that his actions had given their kids pathetic ideas of what it means to be a hero or even an adult. He launched back with, "I am not a role model." To the contrary. He was a role model, and a lousy one at that.

Elderly people sometimes slide into despair, believing that their lives no longer matter. This may be because they are removed from more obvious leadership roles that they held in the past. A woman in a nursing home, however, told me about her two roommates, both of whom had died. She said, "They were both very sick. But what a contrast. The first woman complained about everything. She whined about the food and the beds, the nurses and what was or wasn't on television. But my last roommate, Marie, was the gentlest person. Even when she was dying, she'd ask what she could do for me. She was a pleasure to be around. I know I'll die some day probably not far off. But I'm more at peace with that after knowing Marie. She taught me how to die well."

My point is simply this. In one way or another, every human being at some time is called to some type of leadership that can incite greatness in the life of another. Commonly, but erroneously, we are taught that people become great leaders when they add more zeros to the number of followers or to the amount in their bank accounts.

Jesus taught quite the opposite: the greatness of one's leadership is directly proportional to a person's humility. Most of us often don't take the time to think about the quality of the leaders we follow. We follow them out of necessity or expedience. We adhere to their authority because they are our teachers, professors, or bosses at work. We listen because they talk louder and more authoritatively than anyone else at a time when a decision needs to be made. We pay attention to them because we simply don't want to think that hard about which direction to head next.

So who's right? Do we ascend to true leadership? Or do we find greatness as Jesus said, by heading down and not up? Our answer will likely depend on what we believe true greatness to be. Some ideas of greatness result in the destruction, exploitation, or self-aggrandizement of people, rather than the genuine enrichment of human life. "You may get to the top of the ladder," the saying goes, "only to find it was leaning against the wrong wall." The first task, then, is to understand what true greatness is by Jesus' standards, and then to discover how we might attain it.

PARADOXY

What's Great about Greatness?

In Mark 10:35–37 (NRSV) two of Jesus' key disciples, James and John, came to Jesus for an extraordinary favor:

> James and John, the sons of Zebedee, came forward to him and said to him, "Teacher, we want you to do for us whatever we ask of you." And he said to them, "What is it you want me to do for you?" And they said to him, "Grant us to sit, one at your right hand and one at your left, in your glory."

They were asking Jesus for the most prominent places in heaven—to be seated in honored positions. Jockeying for otherworldly status would probably never occur to most of us, unless perhaps we were spending our days with someone whom we thought might have a say in the hierarchy of our afterlife.

What we do have in common with Jesus' disciples is a desire for greatness on *our* terms. The problem was that, according to Jesus in this biblical text, their perception of greatness was shortsighted and shallow. Jesus answered them:

> "You do not know what you are asking. Are you able to drink the cup that I drink, or be baptized with the baptism that I am baptized with?" They replied, "We are able." Then Jesus said to them, "The cup that I drink you will drink; and with the baptism with which I am baptized, you will be baptized; but to sit at my right hand or at my left is not mine to grant, but it is for those for whom it has been prepared."
>
> When the ten heard this, they began to be angry with James and John. So Jesus called them and said to them, "You know that among the Gentiles those whom they recognize as their rulers lord it over them, and their great ones are tyrants over them.

But it is not so among you; but whoever wishes to become great among you must be your servant, and whoever wishes to be first among you must be slave of all. For the Son of Man came not to be served but to serve, and to give his life a ransom for many."

Mark 10:38–45 NRSV

Jesus was explaining to his baffled disciples what true greatness really is. The two who originally asked Jesus for the special favor were as confused as the other ten, who then thought that they were somehow getting slighted, not having been in on the original conversation.

We should not be surprised that they did not understand Jesus sometimes. I freely concede that many things that Jesus taught are hard for me to understand. But this paradox of Jesus is more accessible when we look first at what Jesus was saying greatness is not.

Greatness Is Not . . . Status and Riches

When Jesus says in Mark 10:43, "But whoever wishes to become great among you must be your servant," he is contrasting the privilege his disciples asked for with the humility of a servant, whose lowly status the disciples would have known all too well. Servants and slaves surrounded the disciples in the ancient Greco-Roman Mediterranean world. Slaves possessed neither rights nor riches. The disciples would have known that Jesus was saying, in effect, "Greatness is *not* status and riches."

Note that Jesus is not saying that those with status or wealth might not also be great. There were biblical figures, some whom Jesus acknowledged or quoted as spiritually significant, who had attained status or riches. And Jesus included the rich and the poor among those who needed and often received God's salvation.

Given this, to presume that having status and wealth destroys one's chances for greatness is missing Jesus' point. Still, according to Jesus, there is something about willing, humble servitude, regardless of our station in life, that leads to and exemplifies real greatness.

Greatness Is Not . . . Fame

Another reason I think Jesus chose the metaphor of a servant, even a slave, was to counter his disciples' inference that greatness was about fame. We often confuse those two. At the height of his fame, a friend asked Winston Churchill, "Aren't you impressed that ten thousand people came to hear you speak?" Churchill replied, "Not really. One hundred thousand would come to see me hang."

Perhaps no other era and no culture more than ours has so lauded fame as the supreme characteristic that determines greatness. This is foolishness. Granted, fame is profoundly seductive. And there is nothing especially wrong with fame in itself. But it is absolutely no guarantor of greatness.

Yet contemporary culture has come to equate fame with everything from stately wisdom to heroic courage. In reality, however, the famous are as likely as any to be foolish or cowardly, and perhaps even more so for those who become famous by pouring their entire lives into self-aggrandizing goals.

I'll never forget an incident that occurred when I was staying with a friend in Santa Fe, New Mexico. At that time Santa Fe had become a strange crossroads for long-term quiet residents, artists, adventurous outdoor types, trust-fund kids, and a growing crowd of Hollywood's young rich and famous.

As my friend and I came out of a diner after a late meal, we heard yelling on the other side of the small town square. There were only a few of us in the vicinity when we heard a man screaming, "He stabbed me. Somebody help me!" Then we saw a man run from the scene.

Those of us on the square ran to the man who had screamed and lay bleeding on the ground with several knife wounds. We began to calm him and tried to stop the bleeding. One man telephoned the police and paramedics. A woman who was a nurse told us where to press on the wounds until the paramedics arrived. As we waited for help to arrive, a handsome young man came sauntering out of a local restaurant with a beautiful date. We recognized him as a Hollywood television actor, from a popular (though I thought rather dimwitted) sitcom. He came over to ask us what was happening and, after hearing about it, seemed completely disinterested in helping.

A moment later, news reporters arrived on the scene, having heard the police dispatch from the telephone call regarding the incident. As the reporters jumped from their van, the young actor quickly knelt down along with us next to the man and dramatically tore off his white T-shirt. He began to push aside those of us who were helping the man and used his shirt to hold the man's bleeding wounds. As the cameras and reporters came closer, the actor began to—well, to *act* . . . like he cared and had been on the scene the entire time. He said something predictable like, "As I came out of the bar, I heard the man screaming. I knew I had to act fast, so I began to stop the bleeding."

No one who had been helping really seemed to care who got the credit. But I did sense that we all had a collective desire to inflict some wounds of our own on this young Hollywood bozo. As is often the case, fame and courageous heroism were at opposite ends of the continuum that night. But it would have been hard to convince the news media and their viewing public of that after his performance.

Greatness Is Not . . . Triumph or Power

In his book *On the Anvil*, Max Lucado says of triumph,

> We honor the triumphant. The gallant soldier . . . the determined explorer. . . . The winning athlete. . . . We love triumph. Triumph brings a swell of purpose and meaning. When I'm triumphant, I'm worthy. When I'm triumphant, I count. When I'm triumphant, I'm significant.
>
> Triumph is fleeting, though. Hardly does one taste victory before it is gone. Achieved, yet now history. No one remains champion forever. Time for yet another conquest, another victory.[1]

Many view Alexander the Great as achieving his epithet because he had conquered much of the known world by his late twenties. He was unquestionably unique. But to retain this title of "great" by Jesus' standards, other qualities would also have to count toward his name.

According to popular ideas of greatness, Jesus would likely be considered a loser. Other religious leaders of his day rejected him. The chief priests, scribes, and Pharisees of his day became some of his strongest antagonists. Jesus did not have property, money, or possessions. Although he gained certain local notoriety over his three-year ministry with his disciples, even his closest friends eventually deserted him and no one came to his aid at his time of greatest need—his arrest, trial, and crucifixion.

Jesus did not wield political influence. He reminded everyone, from respected and revered religious leaders to Palestinian Jewish commoners, to "render therefore to Caesar the things that are Caesar's" (Matt. 22:21 NKJV). Even Jesus understood that he needed to submit to certain earthly political powers. In fact, when the Roman governor, Pilate, asked him about political aspirations, he made it clear that, though Jesus was a king, his kingdom was not of this world.

In spite of Jesus' lack of success in any of those arenas, the cross on which he died remains the world's most identifiable symbol. Jesus' claim to have personally conquered death is confirmed by his empty tomb. He has given spiritual, moral, and personal hope for a renewed life to hundreds of millions to this day.

Status, wealth, fame, power, and triumph are not bad in themselves. Sometimes they even accompany true greatness. But Jesus taught that they are never its source or its end. When found with true greatness they are, at best, only its by-product.

Stooping to Greatness

Jesus continued to drive home this principal: "But whoever wishes to become great among you must be your servant, and whoever wishes to be first among you must be slave of all. For the Son of Man came not to be served but to serve, and to give his life a ransom for many" (Mark 10:43–45 NRSV). True greatness comes about by adopting an attitude of humble servanthood. The way up is down.

PARADOXY

Jesus' life was an example of absolute humility that is worthy of imitating. Writing to the Christians at the church at Philippi, St. Paul elaborated on this:

> Your attitude should be the same as that of Christ Jesus: Who, being in very nature God, did not consider equality with God something to be grasped, but made himself nothing, taking the very nature of a servant, being made in human likeness. And being found in appearance as a man, he humbled himself and became obedient to death—even death on a cross.

Philippians 2:5–8

Apparently, the people at Philippi were struggling with this. That's no surprise, since it's hard for any of us to hear that we need to be humble. We can best practice humility by considering others better than ourselves. To many, that principle may sound like a neurosis that therapy can cure. But let's not miss Paul's point. He didn't want us to ignore our own needs and engender some kind of martyr complex. He said, "Each of you should look *not only* to your own interests, but also to the interests of others" (Phil. 2:4, emphasis added).

The difficulty we find in these verses is not simply that we are asked to serve, but that to become humble we must critique our own lives. Raking ourselves over the coals is painful. It means thinking about what we've done or failed to do and then asking if maybe we were, in fact, wrong when we were so sure we were right. It means not using our positions of power or strength to take unfair advantage of situations or people.

Despite the hopes of many in his day, Jesus was not a ruler or reigning political figure. He was a servant. And precisely because of that, he was great. So Jesus repeated throughout his ministry

TALLER WHEN WE BOW

that when we serve, we reign (Mark 10:35–45); when we become little, we become great (Luke 9:48); and when we are humble, we are exalted (Matt. 23:12). We must stoop to greatness.

Can Great Leaders Be Humble Servants . . . Really?

Doesn't leadership require a person to be in charge, bold, and somewhat exalted? Don't leaders have to be at least somehow larger than life to lead effectively? And if they do, isn't Jesus' teaching that true leaders acquire greatness through humility a bit naive?

Those kinds of questions are common responses to Jesus' description of leadership. But they presume that humility is tantamount to having a timid and hesitant personality. They also assume that the opposite of humble servanthood is confidence. Neither of those assumptions is accurate. The opposite of humility is arrogance. Confidence was essential to Jesus' teachings; it is precisely what he modeled in nearly all aspects of his life.

Jesus was a carpenter by trade, not a reclusive bookworm. He regularly challenged the ruling religious elite of his day to public debates in the synagogues and the streets. He defied social customs by associating with women and publicly defended those caught in sexual violations. He befriended Jewish tax collectors and prostitutes, whose camaraderie might have put him in physical danger by those who hated them. Yet he mingled with all classes of people at will. Jesus confronted the religious rules and laws of his day and once even physically tore into merchants and money changers who he believed were defiling the temple. When arrested and brought to trial, while he was still physically bound and had already been beaten, Jesus audaciously dared public

PARADOXY

officials and his accusers to bring any evidence against him that could stand up to genuine legal scrutiny. Nothing about Jesus' life and demeanor indicates that he equated being a humble servant with being faint of heart.

The same holds true for us. Humble servanthood, according to Jesus' life example, must accompany conviction and heart. We do not become a doormat for the sake of Jesus. Rather, we live boldly. We can pursue with fire the passions that God puts in our hearts. God simply wants us to acknowledge that his power, and not ours, brings us greatness. Writing in the nineteenth century, John Ruskin (1819–1900) said, "The first test of a truly great person is humility. I do not mean by humility, doubt of that person's own power. But really great people have a curious feeling that their greatness is not in them, but through them." God becomes great through those who lead by selflessly and passionately serving others.

Greatness Realized

When I was an attorney, my law firm handled many product liability lawsuits, which were filed when a product allegedly injured someone. The most common first line of defense of the manufacturer being sued for the alleged injuries was to point out that, even though the product may have in fact caused an injury to the person, the person was using the product in a way that it was never intended to be used.

The case law for product liability suits is staggering—a witness to just how dense people can be in their use of products. Just read the warning labels on the things that we use from day to day, from aspirin to lawn mowers. Inside my motorcycle helmet is an arrow pointing to the open face mask that reads "This side forward." I don't even want to imagine the circumstances surrounding the lawsuit that created the need for that warning.

Using things according to their intended purposes usually determines whether they will help or harm the user. You can use hedge clippers to cut your hair, but you're likely to get disturbing results. On the other hand, when people use products as their designer intended, the results are often amazing.

Now, apply this rule of intended use to humans. You can degrade a child, beat on her, frustrate and anger her in order to get the results you want. But God did not design humans to treat one another that way. It should not surprise us that when that child grows up, she stands a good chance of being delinquent, bitter, angry, abusive, or perhaps even suicidal and a danger to herself and society.

We hear people say, "I do nice things for others because it makes me feel good." God designed us to be in loving relationships with others, and part of being in loving relationships is learning how to serve. Since we're designed that way, it is no surprise that we feel good when we live that way.

As the ultimate example, Jesus realized cosmic greatness because of his willingness to serve, even to the point of paying the moral and spiritual price for the sins of humanity. The entire universe, Paul says, bows to Jesus' very name because of the restraint he exerted in going to the cross in obedience to the divine plan and out of love for us. He withstood the temptation to resist arrest. He spoke only what he needed to during interrogations. And Jesus never once cried out to be taken off of the cross.

When we follow the life example of Jesus as we were designed to do, God's highest honors come to us as well. He has a unique purpose for each of us. Jesus alludes to this in his reply to a

PARADOXY

request from his disciples. They had asked him to grant them privileged places in heaven:

> "You do not know what you are asking. Are you able to drink the cup that I drink, or be baptized with the baptism that I am baptized with?" They replied, "We are able." Then Jesus said to them, "The cup that I drink you will drink; and with the baptism with which I am baptized, you will be baptized; but to sit at my right hand or at my left is not mine to grant, but it is for those for whom it has been prepared."
>
> Mark 10:38–40 NRSV

Jesus was essentially telling them, "I have my purpose. It is to die for the sins of humanity. But each of you has a purpose that God has designed for your life. You will suffer and die for me, but according to God's plan for *your* life. Pursue that plan, not the greatness itself, and you'll realize God's greatness for you along that way." Our individual purpose will not be identical to that of Jesus or his disciples, but pursuing it will be just as satisfying.

What's So Great about Jesus?

If Jesus is the teacher of greatness and his humility resulted in universal greatness for him, then considering whether he is really great—and consequently really worth following as a leader—seems worthwhile. Someone wisely warned along these lines, "Never go to a doctor whose office plants have died." Jesus never discouraged scrutiny of him and his ministry. On the contrary, he engaged in his ministry openly and publicly, and personally invited people to get to know him by following him.

The writer of the Old Testament book of Psalms acknowledged that personal experience is a unique teacher when placing trust in someone, including God. So, Psalm 34:8 invites us to personally experience God when it says, "Oh, taste and see that the LORD is good; Blessed is the man who trusts in Him!" (NKJV).

So why is Jesus worth heeding? He did not have a formal education or travel more than a hundred miles from his hometown. Jesus never wrote a book. He was never elected to public office. Jesus was poor and spent most of his three-year ministry around those whom aristocrats disdainfully referred to as "the people of the land." Jesus was not popular among other religious teachers of his day. Some of his own family members questioned his sanity.

Yet for all that might characterize Jesus as a failure, his life and teachings have impacted our world deeply, broadly, and undeniably. An anonymous author observed,

Socrates taught for forty years, Plato for fifty, Aristotle for forty, and Jesus for only three. Yet the influence of Christ's three-year ministry infinitely transcends the impact left by the combined 130 years of teaching from these men who were among the greatest philosophers of all antiquity. Jesus painted no pictures; yet some of the finest paintings of Raphael, Michelangelo, and Leonardo da Vinci received their inspiration from Him. Jesus wrote no poetry; but Dante, Milton, and scores of the world's greatest poets were inspired by Him. Jesus composed no music; still Haydn, Handel, Beethoven, Bach, and Mendelssohn reached their highest perfection of melody in the hymns, symphonies, and oratorios they composed in His praise. Every sphere of human greatness has been enriched by this humble Carpenter of Nazareth.[2]

PARADOXY

In his book *The Good Life*, Max Anders records that the French general and warlord Napoleon said of Jesus,

> Alexander, Caesar, Charlemagne, and I myself have founded great empires. . . . But Jesus alone founded His Empire upon love, and to this very day, millions would die for Him. Jesus Christ was more than a man.[3]

It's striking that even many of our own modern heroes find their inspiration in this ancient Jewish teacher. Nobel Peace Prize winner and founder of the Missionaries of Charity hospices in India, Mother Teresa commented on what inspired her work for the poor:

> I'm still convinced . . . that if the work was mine it would die with me. But I knew it was [Christ's] work, . . . in Christ we can do all things. That's why this work has become possible, because we are convinced that it is He, He who is working with us and through us in the poor and for the poor.[4]

Mother Teresa—one of the most revered women of our era—emulated Jesus Christ as *her* impetus, strength, and hero. Our true greatness comes through imitating the humble servanthood of Jesus. He is a worthy example to follow.

Our Failure to Find Greatness

If, as Jesus said, greatness comes through taking on a servant attitude that drives our actions, and if we presume that this greatness is possible, important, and desirable, we still face a serious problem. We all consistently fail to be the humble servants that Jesus called us to be.

I have met some great leaders who I thought were humble. Much of what makes them great is their willingness to admit their shortcomings and failures. I have met others who consider themselves effective and virtually flawless leaders. Some go so far as to presume that they have arrived at humility. Of course, the paradox of taking pride in your humility has the tone of oxymorons like "sanitary landfills" or "civil war." Jesus' paradox of greatness is that we find it in humility. The moment we presume that we've arrived at humility, it evaporates.

Nearly all humans, whether as individuals or as groups, fail in practicing humility toward others. Jesus' disciples failed at it, even after spending nearly three years under his teaching and leadership. That's why Jesus had the intense conversation about humility, as we read in Mark's Gospel. We fail at it as well. In act or in thought, all of us fail to serve others; most of us do so frequently. At home, school, or work, with friends or with strangers, even the kindest of us fail to achieve the greatness God wants for us. We envy and covet the possessions of others. We become jealous and angry. We are treacherous, bitter, and cutthroat. And even when we don't overtly carry out such acts, we think smug, self-righteous thoughts about how at least we don't live as thoughtlessly or immorally as "them."

Our educational and political systems have failed to promote attitudes of humble servanthood. Communism, dictatorships, and capitalism have failed to produce societies of the mutual servanthood that Jesus encouraged. Upon his first trip outside a communist country, Polish political revolutionary and leader Lech Walesa (b. 1943) said in France, "You have riches and freedom here but I feel no sense of faith or direction. You have so many computers, why don't you use them in the search for love?"

Martin Luther King Jr. said of our own nation,

PARADOXY

We have genuflected before the god of science only to find that it has given us the atomic bomb, producing fears and anxieties that science can never mitigate. . . . Our scientific power has outrun our spiritual power. We have guided missiles and misguided men. . . . We shall have to repent in this generation, not so much for the evil deeds of the wicked people, but for the appalling silence of the good people.[5]

The result of our failure to achieve true greatness is twofold: First, we realize that we fail miserably in our attempts at humility or in trying to live like Christ to achieve true greatness. Second, we realize that we do not please God. It was this very idea of human arrogance and self-worship that led St. Paul to say in Romans 3:23, "All have sinned and fall short of the glory of God." He also concluded in that book that the result of sin is spiritual death (see 6:23).

Is there any hope for our condition? Can we who long for it come to know at least some of the greatness that God has intended for us? Clearly, Jesus' answer was yes. Again, Dr. Martin Luther King Jr.: "Only through an inner spiritual transformation do we gain the strength to fight vigorously the evils of the world in a humble and loving spirit."[6] The most profound greatness we can experience has its roots in understanding God's forgiveness for our failure to truly serve others. Where do we see this in Jesus' teachings?

There is a subtle but key insight at the end of Jesus' discussion with his disciples about greatness: "Whoever wishes to become great among you must be your servant, and whoever wishes to be first among you must be slave of all. *For the Son of Man came not to be served but to serve, and to give his life a ransom for many*" (Mark 10:43b–45 NRSV, emphasis added). Jesus is telling them that he is not merely an example; he is a walking sacrifice for all the world, and he makes it possible for us to live with the hope of real greatness. Verse 45 tells us that in his humility Jesus became "a ransom for many." What does this mean? *Ransom*, or redemption, means the required price to secure the release of someone or something held captive or hostage. The ransom, or redemption, is the payment itself.

In the Middle East, archaeologists have found numerous shards of ancient pottery with the ancient Greek word *tetelestai* (meaning "paid") written on them. It was a common form of a receipt given when a person paid a bill or taxes. When Jesus was on the cross, his last word was "*tetelestai*." We often translate it, "It is finished." But actually, it is the same word as the one found on those pieces of pottery—paid. Jesus paid the price to God for our debt of sin.

A pastor paints a vivid word picture in describing a slave auction that occurred in the Southern United States in the 1700s. In the center of a town in New Orleans stood a young black woman who had been made a slave. She was seventeen or eighteen years old and was being sold. She, like so many before and after her, had been taken from her parents. The people in the audience began to tender offers. Eventually, she was turned over to the highest bidder. When he came to take her, she said defiantly, "Well, what are you going to do with me now?" To her stunned surprise, he said, "Give you your freedom." And saying this, he handed her the papers of emancipation.[7]

Ransom is a payment demanded for the release of someone from captivity. Jesus became your ransom and mine. He paid the price on our behalf that we owed to God for our moral and spiritual debts that we could never pay. Jesus' mission in the world was to become a deliberate sacrifice for humanity's failure to be truly

PARADOXY

great. He did what we could not do for ourselves. The Bible tells us repeatedly that it was God's free gift to us and not something that we attain by our own efforts (see Rom. 6:23; Eph. 2:8–9).

We may think free is cheap. But while it didn't cost you and me anything, it cost God the price of seeing his own Son suffer and die. And in what seems like a pitiful irony, he died at our hands—the hands of humans who were indebted to God in the first place, adding insult to injury by putting Jesus on the cross as though he had committed all of our wrongs. Make no mistake. The New Testament does not blame Jews, Romans, or Greeks for the crucifixion of Jesus. The ethnic background of those who scourged, nailed, taunted, or struck Jesus at his arrest and crucifixion was entirely incidental to what mattered. It was done by humankind.

Indeed, I have come to realize that, spiritually, I crucified him. My spiritual track record is one of treachery, arrogance, anger, envy, greed, and lust; I have ignored the needs of others to serve myself more times in my life than not. That is clear evidence that I would have been right there with all of them at the crucifixion, trying to shut this man up before his brutally convicting messages exposed to the world who I really was at my core.

St. Paul describes in the New Testament how we humans habitually exist as "slaves to sin" (see Rom. 7:14). We do the things we don't want to do and don't do the things we want to. Our good works pale compared to the reality that the wealthiest, most advanced societies waste billions of dollars on goods and services while the world suffers in desperation around us. In short, even at our best we fail to achieve the greatness through humility that God wants for us. When left to ourselves, humanity seems addicted to moral and spiritual mediocrity, with rashes of brutality, violence, and staggering selfishness. The tragedy occurs when, despite God's provision for us to be freed from our slavery to sin, we choose not to take God up on that gift. We continue to live in the lockdown of our destructive habits, our addictions, and our narcissism.

Until we acknowledge Jesus Christ as Lord, we are all on that slavery block, enslaved to self-centered living. God wants to take you and me by the hand, lead us away from the slave market, and say, "You're free to go. You never have to return here again. I've paid your ransom with the price of my Son." That release leaves us with the freedom to lead, with nothing to prove. We have nothing to earn from God, nothing to gain through arrogance. We can become the servants that Jesus called his disciples to be. Through Jesus Christ, we have the possibility of discovering God's true greatness in each of us.

Meditation

Preachers often tell the story about a pastor who substituted for a Sunday school teacher of a class of little boys. The pastor began the class by asking, "What do you think Jesus was like?" The pastor anticipated an answer like, "Jesus was a good person," or "He was God."

Instead, one little boy raised his hand and said, "I think Jesus was like our Sunday school teacher."

Lord God, make that true of me.

PARADOXY

9: **The Life You've Been Looking For**

Die to Live

Those who want to save their life will lose it, and those who lose their life for my sake will find it.

Jesus

He who has a why to live can bear almost any how.

Friedrich Nietzsche

Several people have told me that their twenties amounted to some of their most confusing and difficult years. That surprised them since our twenty-first-century Western culture so often portrays twentysomethings as having the most fun. But during that decade, people have just entered adulthood and are still figuring out their place. Bewilderment and seeking, rather than fun and excitement, more likely characterize the lives of millions of people in their twenties.

If left unchecked, that same confusion and seeking can set the course for our thirties, forties, and so on, down a road of heart-numbing boredom and just getting by in meaningless careers and lackluster marriages. Unless we pay attention, we can begin a life without meaning and we will hardly even notice.

My twenties were some of my most directionless times. That was not all bad. I traveled off and on for a couple of years throughout Europe, the Mediterranean, and all around the United States. I trekked until my money ran out. Then I would return to my hometown in Illinois where I worked in a variety of jobs for a large industrial credit union that helped pay my way through undergraduate university.

I graduated from college with a Bachelor of Arts in European history. However, I was told that in the job market, this is a little like having a pink belt in karate. I eventually decided to apply to some graduate schools. In the meantime, the credit union assigned me to a bank teller position. I've always thought that overseeing people's food and their money are two of the most dangerous jobs, since they likely constitute the two things that people become the most territorial about—with the possible exception of sex, and I'm not sure what that job would involve.

After several months as a bank teller, I had about all I could take. I often worked at branch offices in malls, where I would stand for several hours listening to mall music and transacting hundreds of deposits and withdrawals for junior high mall rats and zombified suburbanites. I had become surly and, frankly, had come to pity the people who came to my window to do business.

One Saturday afternoon, a middle-aged, rather wilted-looking woman came up to my window. She fumbled through her purse, taking her time to pull out a ragged transaction slip. She tried without success to explain to me what she wanted, and I responded with increasing impatience. After taking four or five minutes of my "valuable time," she said with a faint impression of hurt in her voice, "You know, you're not a very nice person."

She stunned me with her directness, though it had a different effect than the enchanting, "Hey, what the @!# have you people done with my money?!" with which customers so often assailed me. I looked the woman hard in the eyes. I was not mad. I actually appreciated her honesty, and it convicted me in the way that only such straightforward sincerity can.

After a cool fifteen seconds or so, I spoke. "You know what? You're right. I'm not a very nice person. I'm not very nice because I hate this job. I hate this mall. I've got a splitting headache from this sappy music and these fluorescent lights, and I'm tired of shuffling money around for junior highers."

Her tone changed. She looked at me with compassion and asked, "Why don't you quit?"

I paused so briefly it surprised me, before responding, "That's a good call," I said. "I think I will."

I finished her transaction, walked to the manager's office, and very kindly told him with great relief in my voice, "Keith, this is my last week. I'm quitting." It felt good, like I had really decided to live again.

I knew exactly what I wanted to do when I went home that evening. I rifled through some papers in a drawer until I found a phone number of a friend in Jackson Hole, Wyoming. I called him and told him that, before starting graduate school, I hoped to sojourn west for several months to guide whitewater rafts down any river that I could. He gave me the number of a local rafting company. I called early the next day. The man on the other end sounded dry and a bit jaded. Still, I told him I wanted to come out to work for him. He told me a lot of people wanted those jobs, but he thought he might have room for a couple more that summer. Naturally, I took that as a firm job offer, loaded up my VW bug, and drove across the country. The next several months became a great adventure of working as a whitewater raft guide down rivers in the western United States, making new friends that have lasted a lifetime, and living again like life really mattered.

Existing versus Living?

Humans have an unquenchable desire to live. I don't mean merely to survive; God has already hardwired us with that instinct. But we have something more—a yearning to really live. It is not enough to get up in the morning to go to unbearable jobs, drive monotonous commutes, come home to bitter spouses, take no vacations, endure thankless children, long for romantic lovers, and experience absolutely no meaning in this existence. We know that we *must* have more if we are to avoid the tragedy of a wasted life.

So we seek meaning in how we live. We live for the weekends and for our children, for hobbies and for workouts. We try to find meaning in new friends and familiar traditions. We search for significance in fame, wealth, personal advancement, self-improvement, status, and even in immortality.

The pitiful irony about our insatiable efforts is that they often cause us to flash past what we seek, like a car passing fence posts at 150 miles per hour. We intently look to the future as we bypass the present. We rush to grow up and then we long to be young again. We ruin our health to gain our wealth. Then we spend all

PARADOXY

that we've gained to become well again. Some choose paths of hedonism, living as if they will never die, only to find in the end that they never lived for anything that mattered or endured.

All of us mean well when we press on relentlessly to find significance. But our hard work frequently directs us to conflicting goals. I think it was Erma Bombeck who observed a few years ago that the year's best-selling genre of books had been cookbooks, with *diet* books coming in at a close second. We're learning not to eat what we just learned to cook. We want to have great bodies but also to satisfy our every craving. We want fame, and when we get it, we demand privacy. We want to live in cities where the action is, and then we complain about the traffic and noise, soon longing for the quiet country with sunny gardens and clean air. We strive for the highest positions and then spend years in costly professional therapy to help us cope with the stress of being in charge.

Our desires to find self-fulfillment lead us to focus on precisely what Jesus warned against—self-preoccupation. Pop psychology at the close of the twentieth century insisted that the sense of personal emptiness that so many experience in Western culture and that drives us to find real meaning would be remedied if only we'd learn to love ourselves. But so often that claim is a thinly disguised excuse for indulging ourselves even more. So we believe Madison Avenue's television commercials that tell us things like "you're worth it," "you deserve it," and "you've earned it." But increasing global awareness has shown us how shallow that mindset is. Billions in the world work as hard if not harder than any of us in the West and often under much harsher conditions, yet they get no break—today or any other day. We in the West want to give ourselves permission to live selfishly, while millions around us suffer in poverty and desperation.

Our efforts to live more fully often lead us in directions opposite from those we hoped to go in the first place. We party our way into excesses of alcohol and drug abuse. We cheat our way into adulterous relationships. We hoard wealth and material gain until we obsess, constantly in paranoid states over how to hold on to it, lest we lose it all. Then in efforts to give our children everything that we think we missed out on, we give them too much too soon and unwittingly teach them the lousy lesson that they never need to delay gratification. Then we wonder why, in their teens, they end up directionless, unfulfilled, and in a disturbingly growing number of cases, suicidal.

We have made cultural icons of the children of the wealthy, who live in luxury they did not earn and houses they did not build. We make celebrities of those with vacuous personalities and no achievements, who, rather than being grateful, whine and demand more with an air of entitlement that only a good stiff tragedy will likely remedy. Then when they suffer those tragedies, we put them back on the air for a "where are they now" interview and gloat at how well we've done compared to them.

Yet both the actors and the audience of those dramas are pathetic. Both mock the preciousness of people. We watch their shows until the commercial comes on for the child whom we could help with just fifty cents a day. She comes into our homes via our televisions, suffering quietly for just a few seconds before we hear the words, "Won't you pick up the telephone and help, right now—?" *Click*, we change the channel. What is it inside us that avoids the gut-wrenching reality of the less fortunate? Those of us who have the incredible opportunities of the privileged have chosen to create a holocaust of squander.

PARADOXY

Get a Life

In Jesus' day, slaves, gladiators, children, royalty, widows, philosophers, Pharisees, farmers, and fishermen all longed for meaningful lives, just as their modern counterparts do. Providing meaning in our lives was one of Jesus' highest priorities. In John 10:10 he said, "I came to give life—life in all its fullness" (ICB).

Like the rest of Jesus' paradoxes, his offer of a full life comes through an apparent contradiction. But in studying the paradox of dying to live, we find that a person can learn to live out all the other paradoxes of Jesus and still miss the real essence of what Jesus taught. Ultimately, this paradox points us not to a way of life but to the paradox teller himself.

In Matthew 16:24–26 (NRSV), Jesus spelled out this final paradox that clearly goes to the core of his teachings:

> If any want to become my followers, let them deny themselves and take up their cross and follow me. For those who want to save their life will lose it, and those who lose their life for my sake will find it. For what will it profit them if they gain the whole world but forfeit their life? Or what will they give in return for their life?

This same basic teaching is also found in the book of John, where Jesus told this to a group of Greeks (apparently converted to Judaism) who wanted to see Jesus. Like the disciples, these Gentile followers of Jesus also longed for meaning and significance.

Whether close disciples or distant fans, Jesus told them all the same thing: the truly fulfilled life is not found in the pot at the end of the rainbow, striking it rich, seeing years of work pay off, or any of the other ideas by which we often define success. Instead,

Jesus said that real fulfillment comes from a radical denial of our selfishness coupled with a surrender of our lives to God.

Bible scholar Raymond Brown explains how Jesus' comment in John 12:25—"The man who loves his life will lose it, while the man who hates his life in this world will keep it for eternal life"—was both a directive to anyone who would follow him and an example of self-sacrifice and mission for us to emulate. Brown writes, "Jesus had to die in order to bring others to life; now we see that the followers of Jesus cannot escape death any more than the master, but must pass through death to their own eternal life."[1]

At the root of this paradox resides three foundational principles that reveal powerful truths.

Wanting What We Need

Jesus' first foundational principle in this paradox is found in his words, "the person who loves his life will lose it." He is in effect telling those who want to follow him, "You need to discern what is really important. And what you want may very well not coincide with what you need." This first principle is about missing the point. We become fixated on our habitual ways of going through life, focusing all our energies on small-minded projects or misguided ambitions. Endless hours of mediocre television shows wash over millions who sit in La-Z-Boy lounge chairs. And all the while we miss out on the most obvious and crucial things about life. The Old Testament prophet Isaiah warns,

> Why spend money on what is not bread,
> and your labor on what does not satisfy?

PARADOXY

Listen, listen to me, and eat what is good,
and your soul will delight in the richest of fare.
Give ear and come to me;
hear me, that your soul may live.

Isaiah 55:2–3

Sometimes we miss God's best for us by purposely turning the wrong directions. Other times, our laziness and neglect mislead us. Wonderful opportunities for change, improved relationships, and healthier living can come our way. But rather than seize them, we bury ourselves in the mindless columns of fashion magazines. We listen to TV news commentators drone on endlessly about the minutia of their respective fields. We tell our loved ones to be quiet so that we can hear another car salesman plug his sedans or an athlete cuss out the referee. But at those very moments, truly significant events transpire all around. Children are waiting to play a game with us. A friend is waiting for our call. Our lover is waiting to get flowers with a beautiful note "just because." Our jobs are waiting to be done with excellence. Our bodies are screaming at us to get off the couch and pump the cholesterol out of our arteries. And God is waiting for a few quiet minutes of prayer that we promised yesterday, and the day before that, and the day before that. All of those things hold out the promise of meaningful life. *And we miss them.*

A young woman I know had been estranged from God for many years when the events of September 11, 2001, shook the world. But at the end of that week, she, like millions of others, wanted to draw close to others and to God. She went to a church to hear a word of comfort. The preacher, however, had been doing a series on a particular topic. When she came that Sunday, he didn't diverge from it. She sat in church that day and wept.

I suspect that the pastor may have had various reasons for not talking about the bombings, not the least of which may have been feelings of inadequacy. I was the senior minister of a large church at the time, and I know how hard it was for me to talk about those events, especially in their immediate wake. But I also think that the *only* reason a pastor could ignore those historic terrorist acts on American soil was because he was preaching to a culture in which ignoring the obvious frequently seems to provide the most immediate comfort. We somehow convince ourselves that, like the families of alcoholics, we can tiptoe around the elephant in the middle of the room, and no one will be the wiser.

But Jesus clearly wants us to keep a sharper focus. He calls us to shake ourselves out of our preoccupied stupors. We who want to follow him will find the fulfillment we've been looking for only when we make a radical break from daily habits that comfort us in their familiarity. Real spiritual change happens when first we resolve to lose ourselves in the mystery of God's plans and purposes for us and then act on that resolution.

Seeking fulfillment in self-serving, self-centered ways will no more bring ultimate satisfaction than drinking salt water will quench our thirst. My wife is a flight attendant, so we've had several opportunities to travel to various destinations. Though I never really had a desire to go to Hawaii growing up, my first visit to that remote island chain was the result of a spur-of-the-moment invitation. Since then, I have returned many times, and it has become a favorite place.

I am dumbstruck by its lilting beauty, fascinating Polynesian culture and history, and its deep azure water, clear and full of amazing sea life. But as I have stood on the islands' magnificent mountains and looked out on the water, pondering that it is the most distant archipelago from any major land mass, I have

PARADOXY

wondered about the ships and their crews who over the years were lost in those deceptively gorgeous waters.

When they ran out of water to drink and their thirst consumed them, in desperation they drank from what looked so refreshing and surrounded them as far as they could see. But ocean water contains many times more salt than the human body can tolerate at one time. The tragic irony for those who drink it in delirious thirst is that it dehydrates them. The more salt water one drinks, the thirstier he or she becomes. The person dies of thirst.

Searching for fulfillment through self-service is like trying to quench our desperate thirst with salt water, but each time we take a drink, we demonstrate we have not learned to want what we really need. Once again, our choice is spiritually deadly. Augustine said, "Before God can deliver us from ourselves we must undeceive ourselves." That's why it's so critical to listen to the wisdom of Jesus' teaching: "The person who loves his life will lose it."

Abandon Selfishness and Gain Real Life

Jesus' second fundamental principle for true life says, "Those who hate their life in this world will keep it for eternal life" (John 12:25 NRSV). *Hate* my life to gain it? How can anyone be mentally, emotionally, or spiritually healthy and hate his or her life? Jesus hammers his listeners with language that would send contemporary client-centered, believe-in-yourself-you-can-do-it therapists reeling. This principle seems destructively counterintuitive.

But Jesus' use of "love" and "hate" shows an extreme contrast of how our inordinate love of life on *our* terms, rather than God's, can lead to spiritually fatal consequences. Matthew Henry described it as a man hugging himself to death. We can indulge our every animal appetite with absolutely no discretion and thereby shorten our days.

Conversely, Jesus suggests that his disciples hate their lives. He calls us to despise self-indulgences that we think will give us true life, but which are really futile and inadequate to fulfill us; especially compared to the fulfillment we find when we embrace life from Jesus' vantage point. St. Paul said in this regard, "But I do not count my life of any value to myself, if only I may finish my course and the ministry that I received from the Lord Jesus, to testify to the good news of God's grace" (Acts 20:24 NRSV).

Jesus is not some life-negating misanthrope. In fact, affirming our love of life is precisely what he is intent on communicating. He is speaking in hyperbole—strong, overstated language used to hit people on the head with the proverbial two-by-four. Jesus is deadly serious about this point and wants his listeners to gain the right focus. He is speaking to those who have had it wrong when they thought they had it right.

When he tells us that if we hate our lives we will keep them, Jesus is saying that the *ways* we often try to gain fulfilled lives are counterproductive, even deadly. To win is sometimes to lose. And the opposite is similarly true—to veer away from one's own selfish desires and lifestyles allows us to find ourselves in ways that we never have.

Becoming Jesus' Disciple Means Being Where He Is

John 12:26 concludes Jesus' third foundational principle for losing and finding life: "Whoever serves me must follow me; and

PARADOXY

where I am, my servant also will be. My Father will honor the one who serves me."

In the 1960s in the United States, many people began to leave spouses, families, jobs, homes, and commitments of all kinds to go out and "find themselves." For the most part, I don't think it worked. They might have had a good time, but the whereabouts of most of their "selves" remained at large. Jesus tells us that we find ourselves when we go where he goes. And where did Jesus go? Among other places, to the poor, the sick, the lost, the lonely, the oppressed, the discouraged, and the captive. He frequently hung out with the unwanted, the immobile, the irreverent, and the interracial. Jesus seemed to avoid the bureaucratic, the rigid, the cold- and hard-hearted, the arrogant, and the duplicitous. In essence, Jesus befriended those who were spiritually and often physically and emotionally broken, and who were more than willing to admit it and ask for help.

Going to the places that Jesus went is often not glorious, romantic, or sensational. In fact, we may find ourselves in places of real discomfort and even danger. However, when we are willing to go to those places, we become like the grain of wheat that is buried in the ground—a patch of ground that God has set aside for us. There, we experience new life filled with unimaginable possibilities. There, we find God using us. What we thought was our sacrifice turns out to be our windfall.

The point is just this: only those who take up with Jesus, following him in true discipleship, will find themselves on his mission. But it is on that journey that our lives become worth living. We can see people with God's balance of compassion and justice only if we see them through Jesus' eyes.

The Family You've Always Needed

We all need others at some time. "No man is an island," wrote John Donne in the seventeenth century. He was right. Some of us are more independent than others. Some are even annoyed by the neediness or clinginess of others. But at some point in our lives, all of us need one other person whom we can trust or confide in when life gets really tough. Our families are those whom our laws say our property goes to when we die (unless we designate otherwise). Our families are those whom we should be able to count on in infancy and old age to take care of us. While our families are almost never ideal, they are critically necessary for our quality of life.

When we follow Jesus as his disciples, he tells us that we become part of God's divine family. John 12:26 says, "My Father will honor the one who serves me." Jesus made various references to God during his three-year ministry, but here he spoke of God as his "Father." It was a family reference, and it says that God honors those who follow Jesus as Lord. We can also call him Father.

This is certainly not to say that all of our family experiences are good ones. Clearly they are not. This is no less true for the big family that is the Christian church. I have not liked, let alone loved, every Christian I have met. And being a Christian in a secular society can at times also be uncomfortable, given that many people are anywhere from indifferent to antagonistic toward Christianity and its followers. But this only drives Jesus' point home further. When we follow him in discipleship, when we lose our lives in Jesus, it becomes clear: As Christians we are not in this alone. We are part of a family that God oversees as a loving parent.

Author Carlyle Marney wrote in *The Carpenter's Son*,

At the cross there is no place for observers. There is no detached ground; there are no uninvolved ones. We are caught here. . . . You are in it: the drama of the redemption of the world. But you are not alone—there are no single crosses anywhere, anymore. All our crosses participate in Jesus' cross.[2]

As disciples of Jesus, we enter into a relationship with God as children of God, and we become part of God's honored family.

God's Family

The family of God is broad and varied. I have always been struck that four separate biographical accounts of Jesus survive in the New Testament books of Matthew, Mark, Luke, and John. Apparently, God enjoys a variety of human personalities and the diverse understandings of Jesus those personalities bring to us.

Jesus himself met with and ministered to people from many different cultures and welcomed them all. Sometimes his associations created scandalous situations. Jesus once began a conversation with a Samaritan woman who was getting some water from a well (see John 4). The Jerusalem Jews typically would not speak to the Samaritans, who were considered ritualistically impure from birth. Moreover, men usually did not speak to women alone. Then there were the Old Testament stories of Jewish patriarchs like Isaac and Jacob who had met their wives at wells, sure to carry additional latent meaning for Jews observing this scene. And one more strike: this woman turned out to be a person who had been married and divorced five times.

All these things made Jesus' meeting with her a clear break from the religious piety of other "respectable, God-fearing" people. The ambiguity of the circumstance could easily have been viewed as Jesus flirting with a woman with a bad reputation. But he didn't care how it looked. He cared about her.

Initially, Jesus had asked her for a drink of water. Recognizing the social and religious risk Jesus was taking, the woman responded with surprise, saying "How is it that you ask *me* for a drink?"

But then Jesus replied,

> If you knew the gift of God, and who it is that is saying to you, "Give me a drink," you would have asked him, and he would have given you living water. . . . Everyone who drinks of this water will be thirsty again, but those who drink of the water that I will give them will never be thirsty. The water that I will give will become in them a spring of water gushing up to eternal life.
>
> John 4:10, 13–14 NRSV

Jesus went on to talk to her about her past relationships. He offered to quench the thirst that she obviously had—not her physical thirst, but her spiritual thirst. Jesus offered her genuine satisfaction; not the temporary satisfaction she had intermittently found in her relationships with men, but ongoing and everlasting satisfaction that she could find only in God through Jesus.

The woman was so deeply moved by Jesus' compassion and presence that she returned to her village and talked about him to everyone she could find. She wanted to bring them back to meet him. Without even explicitly saying it, she had become a follower of Jesus and had joined God's family. John concludes that event, saying, "Many Samaritans from that city believed in [Jesus] because of the woman's testimony" (John 4:39a NRSV).

Like that woman at the well, the companionship that I have found in others who have come to know Jesus spans the globe. In dozens of cultures in hundreds of cities, many on different continents, I have met people who are followers of Jesus like I am. They bring to Christianity their own unique ways of understanding Jesus. Yet something strangely and wonderfully familiar always resides in them. They know him in the personal way that I do. His forgiveness and sacrifice have touched them, and the example of Jesus and the power of the Holy Spirit have energized them toward a newness of life.

The family of God that we enter when becoming a follower of Jesus gives us the confidence of knowing what really matters for life fulfillment. To be a part of that family, we simply release our former selfish lives and abandon ourselves to God's care.

Why Dying to Self Works

Why is there power in dying to self and living for Jesus Christ? Death to self allows us to give absolute commitment to a cause much larger than our own immediate and fleeting passions. Great things that people do are nearly always accompanied by an equally great willingness to throw one's whole life behind an endeavor.

I met a man in Goa, India, many years ago who was coming from Pakistan to serve in a mission hospital set up to minister to the most hopeless of people on the streets of Calcutta. He had become a Christian, and he spoke about his new discipleship to Jesus Christ with a striking sense of commitment that I rarely see in people in the West. At one point in the conversation, I said to him, "There are a lot of dangers in Calcutta; health risks, robberies. And you may find troubles just because you are Pakistani. You could die there." The man gave me the most gentle and sincere smile, and said, "Not a problem. I died before I got here." When we die to ourselves, even when it's painful, we gain the lives we always wanted, the lives we really needed. Then little else seems to matter, because we find what we were seeking in the first place—lives filled with meaning, hope, and contentment.

I have heard an account of a man and his companion traveling across the Himalayan Mountains when they lost their way in a severe snowstorm. They were fighting to stay alive and keep going when they literally stumbled over a man who was half dead in the snow. The man's companion refused to stop and so continued on alone. The other man, however, put the dying man on his shoulders to carry him as best he could. Through his struggling and the mutual warmth of their bodies, he began to warm up, as did the unconscious man. Soon both of them were able to walk together. But before reaching the village, they found, frozen to death in the snow, the former companion who had tried to continue on his own. The paradox that Jesus taught is true: "For those who want to save their life will lose it, and those who lose their life for my sake will save it" (Luke 9:24 NRSV).

Olympic athletes train for decades for a few moments in the arena where all of their years of work and strength are tested. But their fervor is not just about them. It's about the country they represent, the millions of people that their country's flag symbolizes. An athlete thinks about that as she vaults over the horse or as he launches down a track.

St. Paul uses the athlete in a graphic analogy:

Do you not know that in a race all the runners run, but only one gets the prize? Run in such a way as to get the prize. Everyone

PARADOXY

who competes in the games goes into strict training. They do it to get a crown that will not last; but we do it to get a crown that will last forever. Therefore I do not run like a man running aimlessly; I do not fight like a man beating the air. No, I beat my body and make it my slave so that after I have preached to others, I myself will not be disqualified for the prize.

1 Corinthians 9:24–27

In ancient times, the Greeks had two famous national athletic games, the Olympic and the Isthmian games. The Isthmian games were held in Corinth. So when St. Paul wrote to the Corinthians in terms of athletic games, they understood it.

The race was always a major event at the games, and its contestants were required to undergo grueling training for months on end. This was the event that Paul used to illustrate the consistent Christian life: "Do you not know that in a race all the runners run, but only one gets the prize?" No one would train so hard for so long without intending to win. Yet out of the large number of runners, only one wins.

The key difference between the athletic races and the Christian "race" is that we do not compete against others but against spiritual, moral, and material things throughout life that become barriers for us. But we run nonetheless, because we run to convey the love of God in word and in deed to other people, seeking to win them over and to reconcile them, in their broken relationships, to God. That's why Paul is so intent when he says, "Run in such a way as to get the prize." People's spiritual destinies are at stake in the calling that Jesus gives us. *That* is what makes the discipline of dying to self worth it all.

Why Self-Denial Is So Difficult

If all we have to do to find real fulfillment is become followers of Jesus, then why don't more people do it? I suspect there are many reasons. But a few pronounced ones come to mind. First, people question Jesus' lordship. I have talked extensively throughout this book about the unparalleled impact that Jesus of Nazareth has had on human history. I have talked about how his own followers deserted him after his death, returning to their old jobs in despair. Then three days later, Jesus' resurrection so transformed them that they all came together again to proclaim that they had seen Jesus alive and well, risen from the dead. They took that message, along with Jesus' other teachings, and turned their known world upside down for the name of Jesus Christ. Most died martyrs' deaths for their claims.

The radical commitment made by Jesus' disciples is an obstacle for many. However, to be ultimately convinced of the reality of his claims, Jesus made it clear that a person must give his or her heart and life over to him, trust him for divine forgiveness, and be willing to die to his or her former self-serving way of life. Jesus said, "Anyone who does not take up his cross and follow me is not worthy of me" (Matt. 10:38a).

Those who question his lordship should honestly ask themselves, "Is my philosophy of life really so great that I have found the insight, gratification, personal power, and all the other attributes that Jesus says come only by living out his paradoxes?" If the answer is "Not really," then consider taking Jesus up on his offer of true life.

The other major reason that people hear Jesus' message but still ignore his claims is because they are afraid of what it might cost them to follow. To those people, I would say a few things. First, there is in fact a cost to following him. Jesus asks for loyalty and commitment in his followers. He stands ready to forgive us when

PARADOXY

we aren't always faithful. But his call to discipleship is a serious matter. On the other hand, to ignore Christ's call is to risk missing out on the fullest life we can have (John 10:10). To ignore Jesus Christ is to risk missing eternal life (John 11:25–26).

Despite the cost of Christian discipleship, consider this. *Every* philosophy or theology of life that you follow will cost you exactly one lifetime's worth of energy. But *not* every way of life holds out the promises of fulfillment and eternal life that the resurrection of Jesus Christ does.

Every person must respond to Jesus' call of losing his or her life in order to gain it. A nonresponse is a choice to reject him. Jesus said in Matthew 12:30, "Whoever is not with me is against me, and whoever does not gather with me scatters" (NRSV). It is critical to take the time to discern what is truly important for a fulfilled life.

My decision to follow Jesus Christ has made all the difference in my life. The message of Jesus has made sense of a world filled with ambiguities. It coincides with how life really is. It has held true. Jesus was realistic about the maladies of humanity and yet offered a plan of hope. His paradoxes provide for a balanced life: as he demands a rigor in discipleship, he offers the freedom that is always available in the forgiving grace and mercy of God.

But Jesus' paradoxes are an ironic path to personal peace. I confess that I often stray from them, and so God's peace fades in and out of my life. Still, in those times that I let go of my demands, my ideas of greatness, and what I presume will bring about the life I want, and I submit to see life through Jesus' eyes, I experience God's profound peace with unmatched clarity. I find the life I've been looking for.

Meditation

O Jesus! meek and humble of heart, Hear me.
From the desire of being esteemed,
    Deliver me, Jesus.
From the desire of being loved . . .
From the desire of being extolled . . .
From the desire of being honored . . .
From the desire of being praised . . .
From the desire of being preferred to others . . .
From the desire of being consulted . . .
From the desire of being approved . . .
From the fear of being humiliated . . .
From the fear of being despised . . .
From the fear of suffering rebukes . . .
From the fear of being calumniated . . .
From the fear of being forgotten . . .
From the fear of being ridiculed . . .
From the fear of being wronged . . .
From the fear of being suspected . . .
That others may be loved more than I,
    Jesus, grant me the grace to desire it.
That others may be esteemed more than I . . .
That, in the opinion of the world,
    others may increase and I may decrease . . .
That others may be chosen and I set aside . . .
That others may be praised and I unnoticed . . .
That others may be preferred to me in everything . . .
That others may become holier than I,
    provided that I may become as holy as I should.

Rafael Cardinal Merry del Val (1865–1930),
Secretary of State for Pope Saint Pius X

PARADOXY

Epilogue

I can smile at parties that I don't want to be at, greet people pleasantly whom I don't particularly care for, and even do a job with apparent pleasure even though I am unhappy doing it. But there's one thing I cannot fake: my relationship to my two boys, who are now eight and ten.

I was terrified of becoming a father. When my wife was pregnant with our first, I called a friend to go to lunch and sounded so desperate over the telephone that he thought I was going to tell him that Jan and I were getting a divorce.

We sat down at a restaurant, and clenching the sides of the table with white knuckles, I told him, "Jeff, Jan and I are going to have a baby."

Jeff smiled and then tipped his head back with a strangely reassuring laugh. "Tom, you are gonna have so much fun." He didn't add what so many parents say: "It will be a lot of work too." Jeff just said, "It will be great."

Jeff was right. My memory about both of my boys' births always comes to me with photographic clarity. Aaron was born with curly red hair. The second he was born, I trailed the attending nurse who swept him away to the next room where she washed him off. He was kicking and yelling on a small table. I stood there watching with an irrepressible grin on my teary face. I couldn't wait to get my hands on him.

The nurse wrapped him up and handed him to me. "Here ya go, Dad," she said, smiling. I just stood there crying, looking at him, and said, "Welcome. You're welcome here, little boy."

Ryan's birth was no less eventful for me. Jan's first labor had been long and uncomfortable. But with Ryan it seemed like it lasted about ten minutes. (Jan would likely dispute this.) When he was born, he was as different from Aaron as could be. His hair was dark and thick, and his attitude was sweet and docile. He would cry only when we tried to wake him up from his coma-like naps. I held him for the first time, looked at his angelic face, and told him, "Welcome, little Ryan. I'm your dad."

I am madly in love with those boys and want to pass on to them the things that have mattered and helped me the most in my life. Without a doubt, embracing the paradoxes of Jesus is one of the most important. I often think about times my sons will need to embrace them when they are older. To make hard times bearable, good times, meaningful, and just for the road ahead, I want them to know . . .

PARADOXY

My Dearest Boys,

I've known you since you were born. I love you in ways that I think you'll only know if you have a son or daughter of your own. There's something important I want to share with you.

Few things in my life have been constant. So, advice rarely has the staying power it should. But this Jesus of Nazareth, he has impressed me. He has changed me from the inside out for the good. In him I've found a God-intoxicated hope in a world that has so many problems and so much pain. Coming to know him personally and then following him has been the most significant experience of my life. I want you to know the hope of Jesus too.

The problem is, I can't experience him for you. You must come to know him for yourselves. You must ask him personally in prayer to be the Master of your lives. But I so believe in both the power of Jesus and his paradoxes that I urge you to look into them deeply. Discover their power. You will see them in light of your own unique experiences, personality, gifts, and passions.

Jesus' teachings can be an encouragement to your hearts and an explanation for your minds. Where answers elude you, the paradoxes of Jesus will nevertheless let you rest in the assurance of God's promises.

Jesus' teachings and ways tilt life on its head. But they're stunningly true. I pray you'll learn them in your hearts and experiences, just as I'm learning them still. See the unseen. Labor to rest. Give to receive. Be enslaved to be free. Find fool's wisdom. Yield to conquer. Serve to reign. Die to live.

Most important, I pray you'll develop a deep, lasting friendship with one of the only constants I've found in life, the Paradox Teller.

Always wanting the best for you . . .

Love,

Your Dad

Notes

Chapter 1 Peace for Restless Souls

1. *Harper's Magazine* (January 1986), quoted in *Christianity Today* 30, no. 4.
2. A. W. Tozer, from Edythe Draper, *Draper's Book of Quotations for the Christian World* (Wheaton: Tyndale, 1992), entries 1263–65.
3. G. Appleton, ed., *Oxford Book of Prayer* (Oxford: Oxford University Press, 1985), 119.

Chapter 2 Take a Load Off Me

The opening quote from Jesus is taken from Matthew 11:28–30.
1. Bombay has since been renamed Mumbai.
2. Eric Hoffer, *The Passionate State of Mind* (Cutchogue, NY: Buccaneer Books, 1955).
3. *USA Today*, November 17, 1986.
4. William L. Shirer, *The Rise and Fall of the Third Reich* (New York: Simon & Schuster, 1960), 249.
5. Ibid.
6. Ibid.
7. Charles Haddon Spurgeon, *The Quotable Spurgeon* (Wheaton: Harold Shaw, 1990).
8. Dietrich Bonhoeffer, *The Cost of Discipleship* (New York: Touchstone, 1995).
9. *Christian Reader* 33, no. 2.

Chapter 3 When Seeing Isn't Believing

The opening quote from Jesus is take from Mark 8:18.
1. Greg Asimakoupoulos, *Leadership* 15, no. 4.
2. Henri J.M. Nouwen, *Leadership* 3, no. 1.
3. Dom Helder Camara, *The Desert Is Fertile* (Maryknoll, NY: Orbis Books, 1974).

Chapter 4 Satisfaction Guaranteed

The opening quote from Jesus is taken from Acts 20:35.

1. *U.S. News & World Report*, April 28, 1996.

2. "The Barna Update," *Giving to Churches Rose Substantially in 2003*, April 2004, http://www.barna.org/FlexPage.aspx?Page=BarnaUpdateNarrow&BarnaUpdateID=161, accessed October 1, 2005.

3. Joel Belz, *WORLD* 17, no. 32 (2002).

4. Ibid.

5. Paul Brand and Philip Yancey, *Fearfully and Wonderfully Made* (1980; repr., Grand Rapids: Zondervan, 1987), 61–2.

6. *Affluenza*, KCTS/Seattle and Oregon Public Broadcasting, 1997.

7. F. B. Meyer, in *Our Daily Walk*. Quoted in *Christianity Today* 33, no. 8.

8. Marilyn Elias, "Psychologists Now Know What Makes People Happy," *USA Today*, http://www.usatoday.com/news/health/2002-12-08-happy-main_x.htm., accessed December 8, 2002.

9. Ibid., quoting University of Illinois psychologist Ed Diener.

10. Author unknown.

11. *Leadership* 4, no. 4.

Chapter 5 Maximum Security Freedom

The opening quote from Jesus is taken from John 8:31–32.

1. D. H. Lawrence, *Studies in Classic American Literature* (London: Penguin Books, 1990), chap. 1.

2. Draper, Edythe, *Draper's Book of Quotations for the Christian World* (Wheaton: Tyndale, 1992), entry 4131.

3. Adapted from a passage in Thomas Merton, *No Man Is an Island* (New York: Harvest/HJB Book Publishers, 1983), 27.

Chapter 6 Against Your Better Judgment

The opening quote from St. Paul is taken from 1 Corinthians 1:18, 25 (NRSV).

1. Ludwig Wittgenstein (1889–1951), Austrian philosopher. "Conversation (1934)" in Rush Rhees, ed., Ludwig Wittgenstein: *Personal Recollections* (Lanham, MD: Rowman & Littlefield, 1981).

Chapter 7 The Power of Positive Weakness

The quote from Jesus is taken from Matthew 18:4.

The quote from St. Paul is taken from 2 Corinthians 12:10 (NIV).

1. *Peoria Journal Star*, April 7, 2002, pp. A1, A16.

2. Mother Teresa of Calcutta (1910–1997).

Chapter 8 Taller When We Bow

The opening quote from Jesus is taken from Mark 10:43b–44 (NRSV).

1. Max Lucado, *On the Anvil* (Carol Stream, IL: Tyndale, 1994).

PARADOXY

2. Paul L. Tan, *Encyclopedia of 7700 Illustrations: Signs of the Times* (Garland, TX: Bible Communications, 1990).

3. Max Anders, *The Good Life* (Nashville, TN: W Publishing, 1983), 34.

4. Malcolm Muggeridge, *Something Beautiful for God: Mother Teresa of Calcutta* (San Francisco: HarperSanFrancisco, 1986).

5. Edward T. Clayton, *Martin Luther King: The Peaceful Warrior* (New York: Pocket Books, 1969).

6. Martin Luther King, Jr., "Transformed Non-conformist," in *Strength to Love* (Philadelphia: Fortress Press, 1963), 23.

7. James Cox, ed., *1989 Ministers Manual* (New York: Harper & Row, 1989), 62.

Chapter 9 The Life You've Been Looking For

The opening quote from Jesus is taken from Matthew 16:25 NRSV.

1. Raymond Brown, *The Gospel According to John I–XIII* (New York: Doubleday, 1966), 474.

2. Carlyle Marney, *The Carpenter's Son* (Wake Forest, NC: Chanticleer Publishing, 1967).

Tom Taylor (Ph.D. candidate, Fuller Theological Seminary; M.Div., Yale Divinity School; J.D., University of Illinois College of Law) is a speaker and the senior pastor of Glenkirk Church in Glendora, California. He is also adjunct professor in the School of Intercultural Studies at Fuller Theological Seminary and author of the award-winning *7 Deadly Lawsuits*. He lives in Southern California with his wife, Jan, and their two boys, Aaron and Ryan.

Visit Tom's website at www.tom-taylor.org.